CRIES FROM THE LONELY ROAD

POETRY FROM THE HEART

WRITTEN AND ILLUSTRATED BY

LESLIE D. FERN

ISBN: 9780646736716 (paperback)
TITLE: CRIES FROM THE LONELY ROAD: Poetry from the Heart
AUTHOR: Fern; Leslie D.
Published through IngramSpark

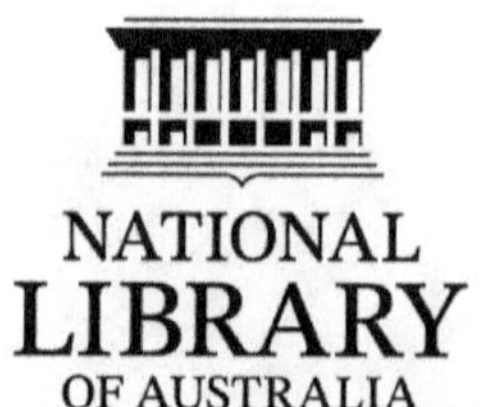

A catalogue record for this book is available from the National Library of Australia

CONTENTS

CONTENTS (CONTINUED)

TABLE OF ILLUSTRATIONS

ABOUT THE AUTHOR AND THE POEMS

I have always had great difficulty asking for help and voicing what is wrong. This difficulty was one that I did not outgrow as I grew older and began to trust once more. I did not know why this was until I was nearing 40 when I was diagnosed with ADHD and autism, a 'disorder of neural development characterized by impaired social interaction and communication, and by restricted and repetitive behaviour.'

While I do not try to use it as an excuse, my upbringing was full of trauma and loss. I was raised in Victoria's foster-care system and experienced physical, emotional and sexual abuse over the first 18 years of my life at the hands of those who were supposed to support and protect me. I was moved to numerous foster placements and ripped from those I loved. I also lost a very close person in my life at a very young age. This left scars that still are evident.

Through a lot of hard work, I discovered that I could express myself through various forms of art including poetry. This expression began the long road of healing. It seems that I have been given a gift with my works and have found that it cannot only help me, but help others as well. I have had a unique journey in life (as have we all) but there are topics that can affect everyone. This is why I have put these poems into book form to share with the world.

So please enjoy these poems and remember that there
are always other people on whom we can turn to for
help. The journey of life was never meant to be trav-
elled alone.
My love to my family and to those I have lost along
the way.

A WARNING TO THE READER

While all care has been taken to provide as honest an
edition as possible, some of these poems refer to sui-
cide, trauma and loss.
These subjects can be triggering for some people.
If you are affected by any of these writings please,
reach out and talk to someone.

Dedicated to the memory of Daniel

1985-2001

Though we had so little time together, I am the person I am today because of your love, friendship and courage. You have never left my thoughts.

ACKNOWLEDGEMENTS

My thanks and love to my mother Brenda, sisters Maggie, Natalie, Leonie and Peggy and my brothers Damian and Jamie. Putting up with this troubled brain is never easy and you have shown strength and wisdom all through the past 20-odd years.
My sincere thanks to Thelma and Laurie (may he be resting in peace) for the love and gentle guidance to a troubled youth fresh out of a major trauma.
A huge thanks to those who proof-read my poetry and offered their opinions and guidance, especially Pip, Hayden and Jamie S.
Finally a big thank you to you, the reader, for taking the opportunity to read this book. It has been a rollercoaster to write and I sincerely hope that you can connect with my words.

THE LONELY BELL

Leslie Fern

I want to fight, yell, scream and cry
Sometimes I cannot tell why
So many emotions seem to build
They keep adding up, until the cup's filled
It's a constant drain, it keeps wearing me down
Choking happiness off without a sound
I keep on trying, I persevere
But my voice is hard for others to hear
I've lost so many friends, and family too
I'm no longer sure what I must do
Anger builds where once there was none
I struggle to be the resilient one
Who I have been my entire life
Through all the pain and the strife
Through decades of this endless hell,
The ringing of this lonely bell,
Cracked and muffled by the weariness of age,
Trapped and frozen within a silvered cage
Does anyone hear my tortured cry,
Do siblings want to fight and try
Or is this just wasted breath
As I march on toward my death.

CRIES FROM THE LONELY ROAD

Leslie Fern

Who am I angry with?
Is it righteous? Is it based on a myth?
The rage that is boiling inside
Makes me want to run and to hide.
But to whom is this anger I direct?
Is it just? Is it correct?
I try my hardest to not internalise
To not let it grow too large inside
Or I could easily hurt myself,
End my life from upon this shelf.
What purpose would this serve
But hurt those who do not deserve
The pain and hurt this leap would cause
So I stop myself, step back and pause.
I long to be happy, I long to be free,
Be all of the things that I desire to be.
I long to have friends to call my own,
To find a job and to live at my home
With friends and family all around,
Where peace and laughter is in every sound.
Instead I am crying from this lonely road
I fear I do not have another mode,
Except to feel this anger and hurt
From the root of my hair down to the dirt.
They feel that they rule my life,
They do not care that this pain is rife.
They act with the impunity of the state,

Where they need not care or commiserate.
They just hurt and abuse my kin,
Believing that I do not deserve to win
The war that rages each and every day
As they force my family away.
To whom can I turn to for help,
When all around is a bed of kelp
That squeezes and strangles without remorse
As they force me onto this course.
I know that they are all against me,
And that I shall never be truly free.

MUSINGS ON MUSIC

Leslie Fern

Music speaks to all who can hear
It spreads to the hearts of all of those near
Builds them up, fills their soul with wonder
Spreads it's melody like the rolling thunder.
It does not know borders, it does not see race,
It crosses oceans at a galactic pace.
It's beat is the pace to which armies march,
It's harmony rises above the tallest arch.
It's bass tones travel through the hardest stone
It's words can provide comfort to those who are
alone.
How blessed we are that music belongs to all,
And comes to you at your beck and call
No matter where in the world you roam,
Music can always lead you home.

PICKING UP THE PIECES

Leslie Fern

Pick up the pieces of a shattered mind

Assemble them, then you will find
The whole is missing a few of the parts.
Where light once shone is now filled with dark
Once broken there is none who can repair the hurt.
Just as a jungle torn down to the dirt
Will never return to the way it once grew,
The shattered mind, torn up, cannot become new.
The pain, at times will never leave
And no matter how much that you will plead
Nothing can ever truly explain
The lifelong damage, this continuing pain.
To those who live with a broken heart,
Whose lives and minds broken from the start,
Try to be strong and trust those you hold dear,
Don't isolate from those who will hear
And care when things have gone wrong,
The road of life is windy and long.
I know what I say is true,
Because I live with a shattered mind too.
I know how hard this life can be,
How it feels you shall never be free,
Know that this world welcomes all,
From the tiny to the tall
Somewhere there is a place to stay
And allow the pain to gently fade.

REMEMBRANCE

Leslie Fern

I was not there when the guns fell silent
With those who fought and died in times most vio-
lent.
I was not there to storm the beaches at dawn,
I have never had mates or comrades to mourn.
I have never had to fear another country would in-
vade,
Or wonder where is the next landing to be made.
I know that there is a debt that nobody can ever clear
I know that there are still those who lost whom they
hold dear.
In November each year, our memories forever set,
And always shall we remember:
Lest we forget

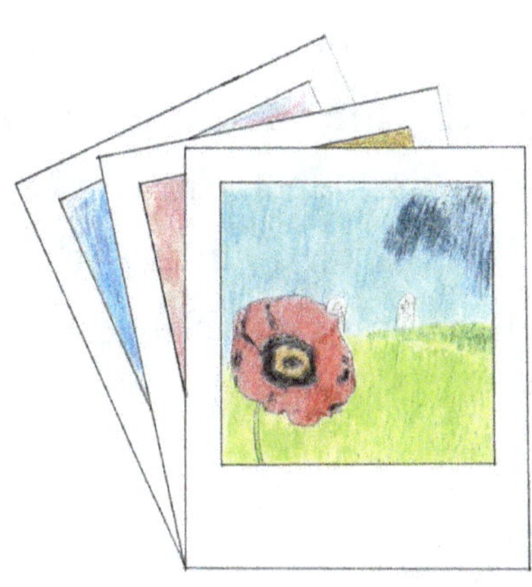

REMINISCING

Leslie Fern

When God made you, he broke the mould.
When you arrived, more precious than gold
You brightened up the darkest of days,
You touched our lives in so many ways.
You never tried to reach for the stars,
You were happiest right where you are.
You were more amazing than grace,
Your sweet voice filled all of the space.
Your cheer lifted those around,
You never yelled to make a sound.
Your laughter was as sweet as honey,
Your friendship was more valued than money.
Your strength came from deep within,
Your heart was free from darkest sin.
I know I am reminiscing, it's true,
But there is nothing that could ever replace
you

SUPERMAN

Leslie Fern

Don't be a superman,
Don't think that you can
Impose your will without control
By using the power of your role.
Be polite, apologise,
Don't accuse me of telling lies
Just because I don't see things your way.
I did not ask to be here this day!
Nor do I give up control,
Like some child's forgotten doll.
Talk to me, negotiate
Don't just make me sit and wait.
You may believe that you know best,
But if you fail the silent test
You run the risk of shutting me down,
For, when my smile becomes a frown,
When I feel the moody blues
That's when I find I have to choose
Whether to fight and get nowhere fast
Or try to move on from my tortured past.

CALLS BEHIND CONCRETE WALLS

Leslie Fern

Lights on, doors slam, go running to the phone,
Dial the number, hit the hash and wonder if they're
home.
Spend the first minute saying hello, fight to say a
word.
Tell them that you love them and hope that you are
heard.
The phone gets passed around so everyone gets a go,
To tell you what is going on and the things that you
should know.
Twelve minutes pass much too fast, soon you hear
the beep,
To tell you that time has ran out, the family begin to
weep.
Calls behind the concrete walls are never easy to
make,
Speaking to those you love whose hands you cannot
take.
Your heart breaks as you hear the pain going down
the line,
Knowing that you cannot help to make everything fi-
ne.
So, if you have one you love in jail and away from
you,
Just know that there is something small that you can
do,
To show them that you love them and tell them that
you care,

Even though they are far away, sometimes who knows
where?
Remember that a single call can really change a day,
And fill a saddened heart, chase their blues away.
So if you get a call from someone far apart,
Always let them know that they are in your heart.

WHERE I BELONG

Leslie Fern

I find that there are times
When I sit to write my rhymes
There come memories that flow
Through my mind, so slow.
They remind me of back when
We sat, laughed and joked, and then
We talked about what was breaking,
Our happiness was out for the taking.
You come to my mind so much these days,
I'm reminded of you in so many ways
Of the life we used to live
Of the joy and love you used to give.
I make what I can of life,
We all face hardship, pain and strife.
It shows that we are unique,
That there are differences in what we seek.
That's why I know you're still there
You always showed me that you care
Now I take the book from the shelf,
Show I can look after this lonely self.
For, then I can show that I am strong,
Then I'll find the place where I belong.

BLUE MARBLE

Leslie Fern

Blue Marble, floating in space
No words can describe your majesty and grace
Your fragile orb seems so small,
As if you would break if you fall.
Very few have seen your magnificent beauty
All are too busy or doing their duty,
But if they take the shortest time
They would be lost in wondrous sublime.
For no mortal could ever replicate
The grandeur of the Great Lakes,
the rugged vista of Victoria Falls
Or the barren peaks where Hillary called,
Your surface teems with life abounds
Covering all of the wild ground,
Filling the air and the seas
From the mighty beasts to the smallest bee.
You are taken for granted and poisoned too
By waste, chemicals and toxic goo,
As if we have nothing to lose
If we cover your azure hue.
With nothing left to lose or win,
killing you is the gravest sin.
So I send out this siren's call
Heed my warning, one and all.
If we destroy our precious home,
There is no other place where we roam.
All of us have a role to play
Each and every single day,
Remember the blue marble upon which we live,
Because our planet cannot give
Us another chance to see
How beautiful this earth can be.

CYCLES

Leslie Fern

The cycle drives like the wind,
Forever constant, never changing,
As people blindly follow
Searching, seeking,
Looking for the path that breaks
Repetition, loops, circles that form
The constant search for meaning
For purpose
For the all-knowing answer
To that endless question:
Why?

FACING THE DARKNESS

Leslie Fern

Facing the darkness, the pain and cold
Travelling though my body and soul.
Taking me back to when I played alone,
When hell existed, the place my home.
I spent years, months, days wearing the mask,
Trying to pretend there is no fear, no pain
That I am happy, feel loved, nurtured,
At peace, strong, brave, carefree.
But masks are meant to protect, not hide
The anguish, the pain, suffering, hurt,
The struggle, the desire, the longing, want
For a kind word, a gentle touch,
The feeling of being wanted, needed loved,
Feelings that have been far from my soul,
For so long, too long.
They are barely echoes, the memories
Of time from long ago when I felt
Happy, loved, nurtured, strong, brave.
Now I feel numb, cold, alone, afraid, weak.
The darkness returns.

HIDDEN BLESSINGS

Leslie Fern

Where is the joy in this world? Who brings all of this
pain?
Is there one at fault? Someone must be to blame.
Is it known who creates the hurt? Is there one to sun?
Is it a daughter that separates herself? Perhaps an ab-
sent son?
I can only control my own acts, not those of anyone
else.
I cannot control others destiny with just a click of a
mouse.
I struggle to allow the thoughts to flow that occur
within my mind.
I know that if I latch on to them that I will begin to
find
My hopes and dreams will fade away, scatted by the
autumn blow
And my future will appear as bleak as winter's snow.
That is why I must learn there are others I can de-
pend.
That is why I know how blessed I am to have you as a
friend.

FINAL GOODBYE

Leslie Fern

It does not matter what I say or do,
Nothing will ever let me talk once more to you.
My acts prevented me from saying goodbye
Instead, I vanished without saying why.
My actions have ruined too many tries,
Torn me away from your laughter and smiles,
Putting me into my version of hell,
A prisoner of this repeating spell.
I keep on trying to do what's right,
To win the race, to fight the good fight,
But then I feel like I am completely alone,
Even though you were as close as the phone.
I struggle and fight my brain each day,
To keep doing things the right way,
But the instant I know I can no longer win,
I may as well throw my life in the bin.
Because there is only one thing I know
That is, this endless rodeo
That rips and tears me apart
To leave me with this broken heart.
So now, I write this final goodbye
To a person that always made me smile.
I wish I was there for the last of your days,
Before death came to lead you away.
Please know that wherever you are,
It does not matter if it is near or far.
You are welcome here, we're never far apart,
And never will you be gone from my heart.

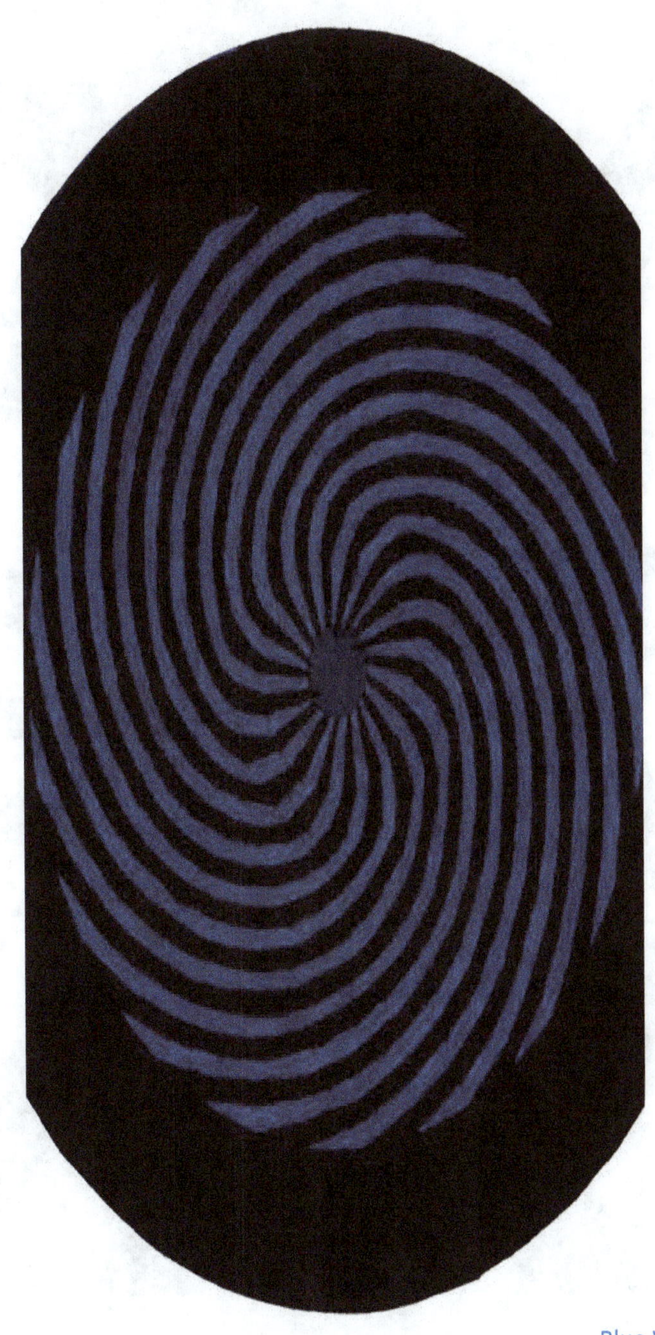

Blue Whirlpool
Pen on Paper by Leslie Fern - 2025

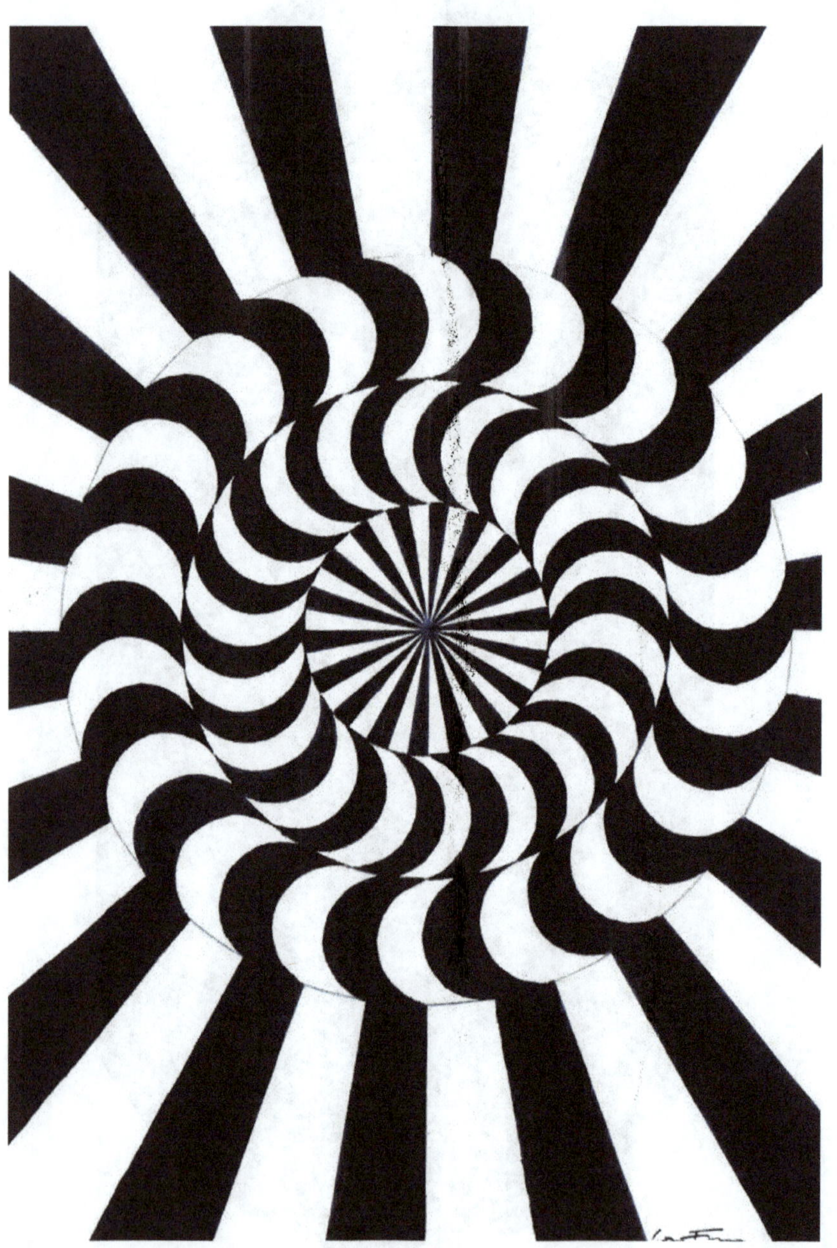

Counter Spirals
Pen on Paper by Leslie Fern - 2025

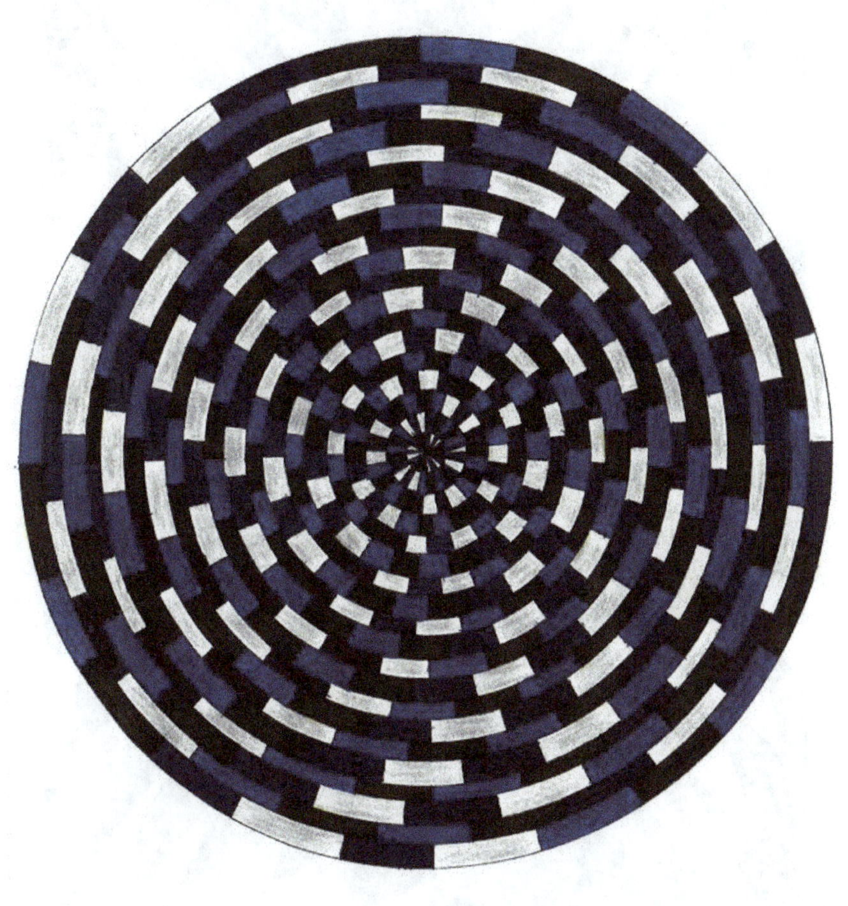

Dark Spirals
Pen on Paper by Leslie Fern - 2025

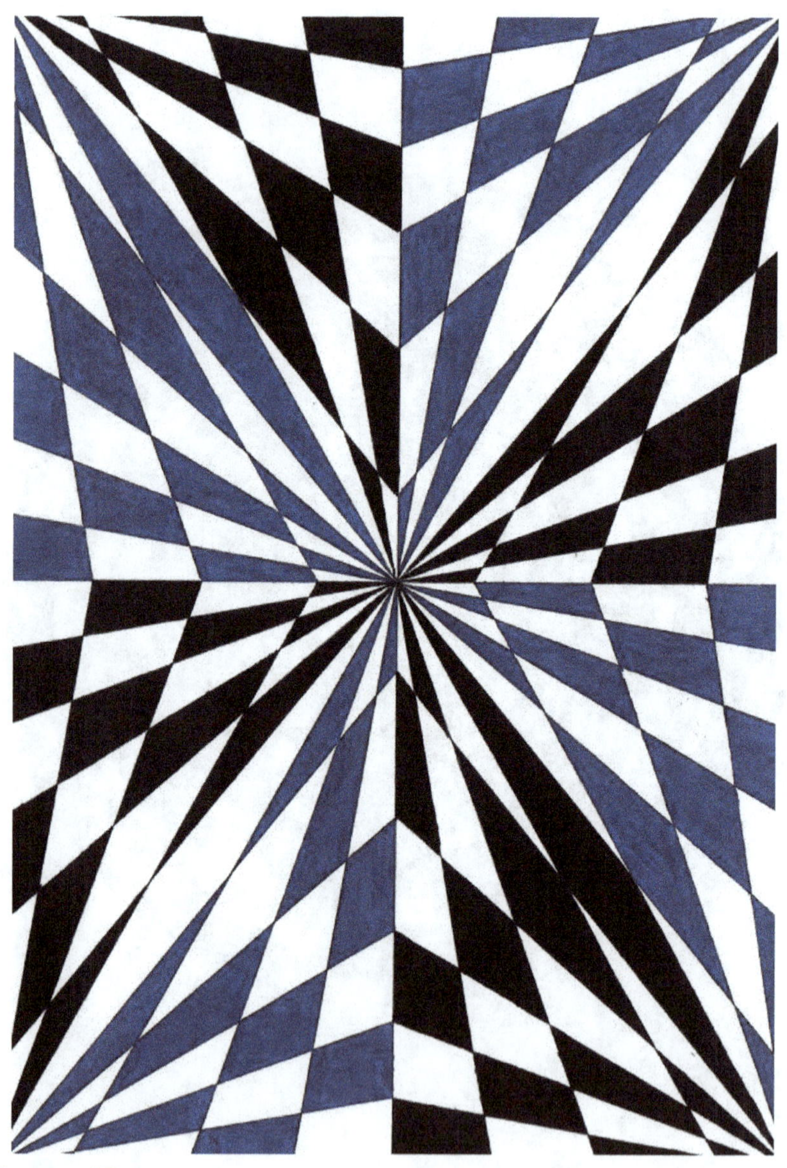

Fractured Plane
Pen on Paper by Leslie Fern - 2025

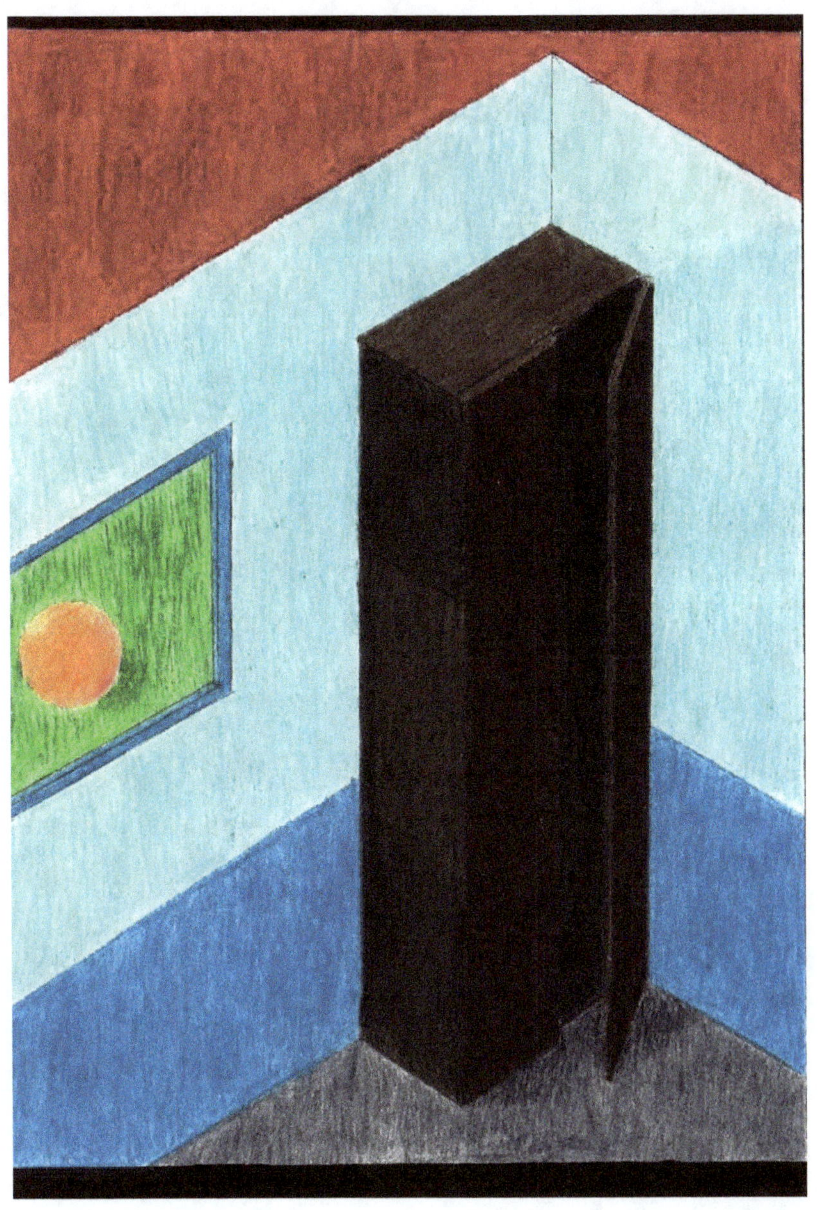

Letting Others In
Pencil on Paper by Leslie Fern - 2025

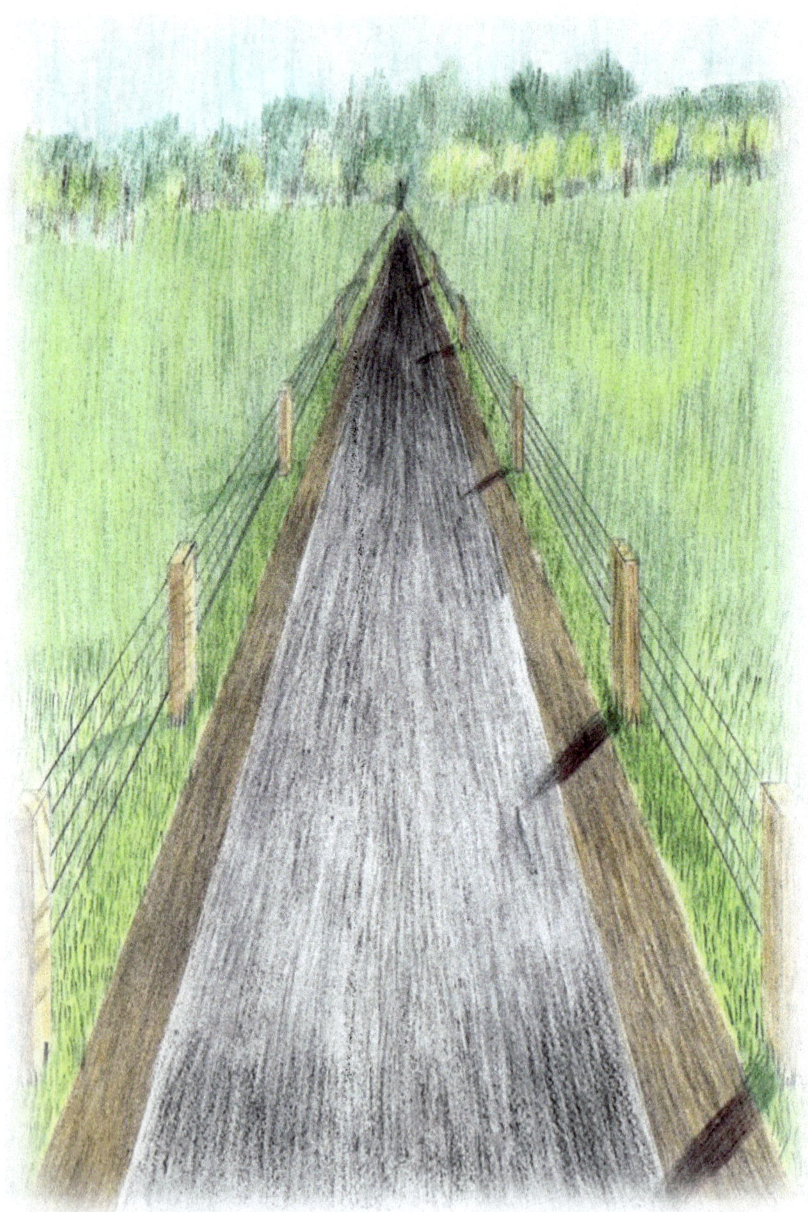

Loneliness
Pencil on Paper by Leslie Fern - 2025

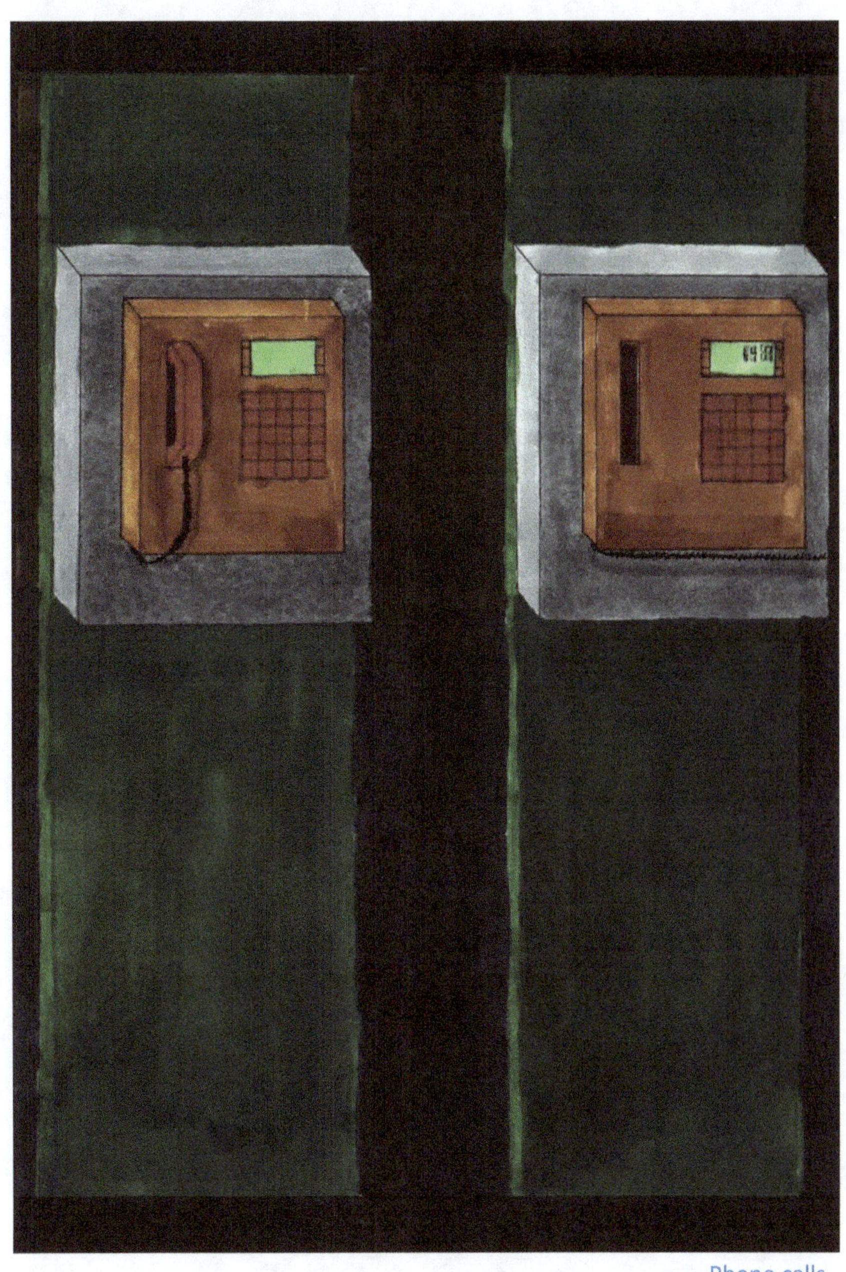

Phone calls
Marker on Paper by Leslie Fern - 2025

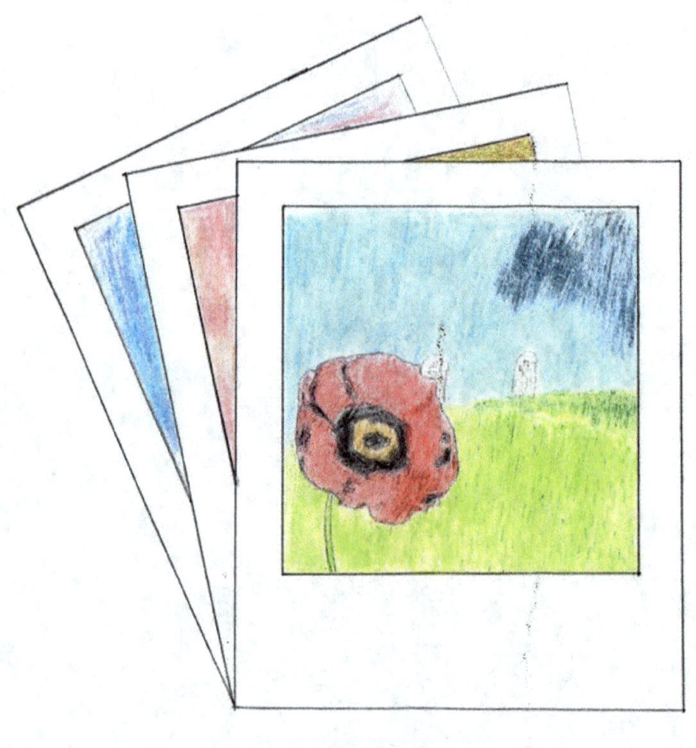

Photographs/Remembrance
Pencil on Paper by Leslie Fern - 2025

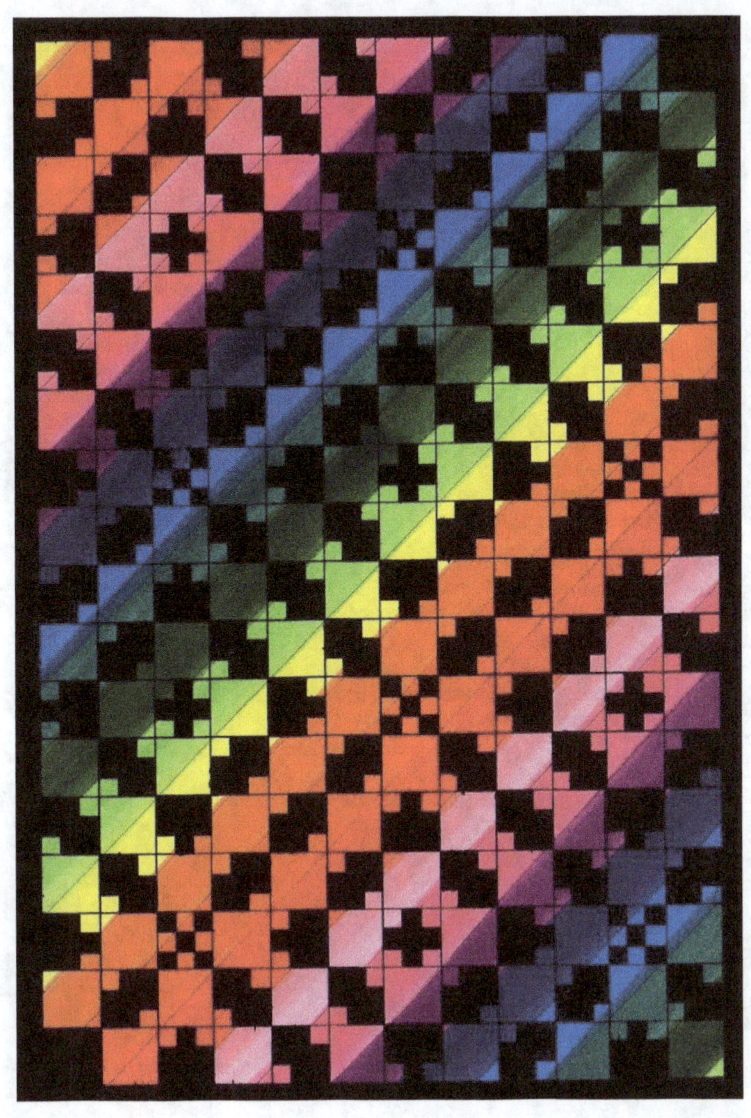

Rainbow Curves
Marker on Paper by Leslie Fern - 2025

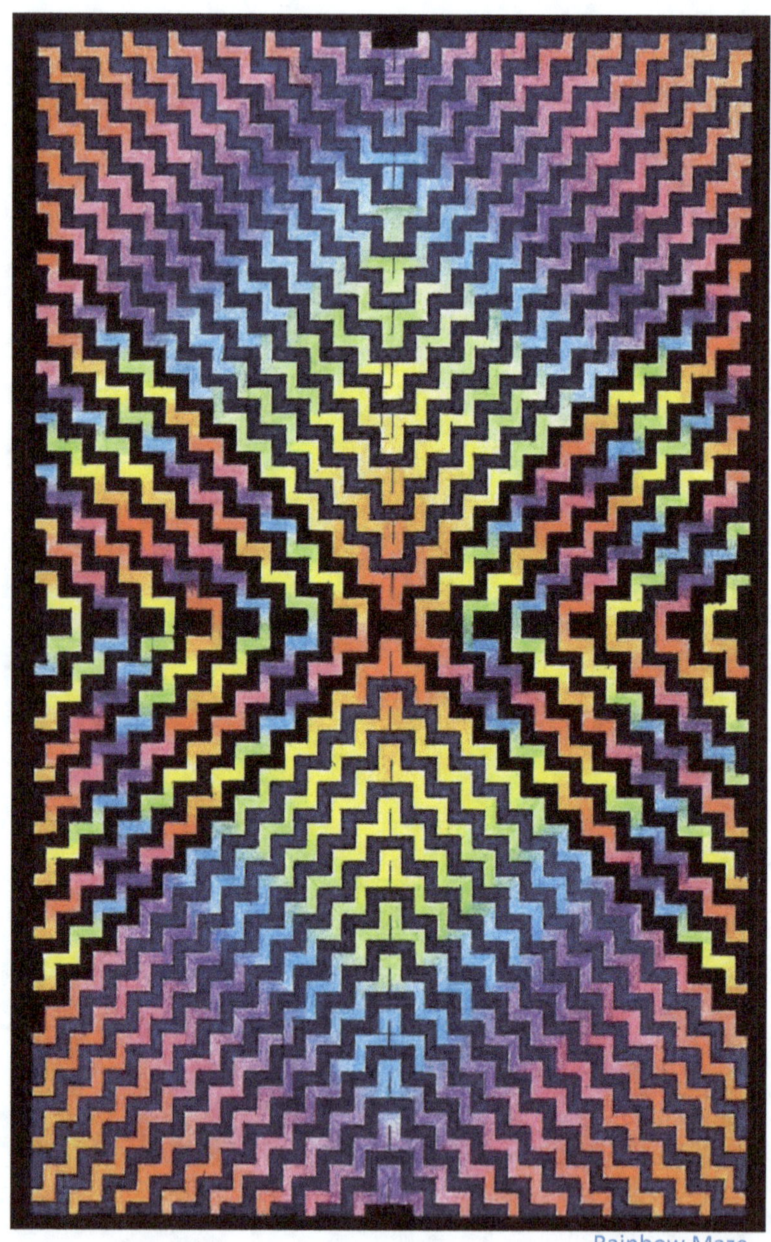

Rainbow Maze
Ink & Pencil on Paper by Leslie Fern - 2025

DESPAIR

Leslie Fern

There's a hollow within me that food cannot fill.
It spreads and clutches it's claws,
Tearing into my soul.
It holds fast and never relents
Fixing pain and anguish through the night and into
the day.
The sun's warmth reaches barely skin deep,
Absorbed by the cold spreading through my core.
Despair and sorrow cloud my thoughts,
Stealing my energy and my will.
Even death's embrace seems a welcome friend
compared to this.

LETTING OTHERS IN

Leslie Fern

The young boy hides beneath the bed, frightened to
the bone
For he has discovered monsters do exist and are hid-
ing in his home.
His carer is one in disguise, nobody sees her true
face,
For not until they are alone does the monster take
her place.
To whom can this young boy turn when the one who
is meant to help
Is the one that he is hiding from, that makes him cry
and yell.
So, he hides and tries to be strong like the man he's
told to be,
And throws his mind open to the dreams, at least
there he can be free.
The man sits upon his bed, his hands upon his lap.
Something lives inside his mind that is taking him
down a dark track.
He knows that he need some help, but to whom can
he turn?
When the monsters are still inside his head and it is
his courage they burn.
Six seconds come sixty then thousands, sill he sits in
terror,
The monsters mock and tease him there, making him
believe his error,

For inside his head they reign supreme and lead him
to the space
Where help never comes to him, instead nightmares
return in its place.
The elder looks back at his life, feeling pride and
what he's overcome.
His hidden torments long revealed, exposed to the
sun.
He no longer fears the night, and his dreams have
now been unveiled,
Chip by chip his armour broke down, exposing his
wounded heart.
The hollows deep inside his soul are no longer alone,
apart.
Help and been freely given and accepted for the gift
it is,
And together the monsters are beaten, new peace can
be his.
All of you who live with memories of monsters under
the bed,
Those that fear the dreams of night whenever they
rest their head.
Know that even though it may feel the evil may never
end,
That monsters still haunt your dreams, the night-
mares that they send.
Know there are people out there who do genuinely
care,
Whose motives and intentions are pure, who dream
of a future where

You no longer fear the night and you can ask for
help.
Where you have a chance to hope and to learn to
love yourself.

MEMORIES

Leslie Fern

Years back when we were young,
When life's journey had just begun,
We explored the world with rapture and glee,
There was nothing we could not be.
Our hopes and lives were intertwined,
My dreams were yours and yours were mine.
We planned and played each and every day,
Never for long were we far away.
People called you my spiritual twin,
Wondered where you stopped and I begin,
Nobody told us we were bad together,
We knew our friendship would last forever.
Your family took me into your home,
They let me make your home my own.
You helped me face the horrors I faced,
Soothed the nightmares that came in their place.
I wondered how I would ever repay
The kindness you showed me every day.
You never wanted a single thing,
Except for the smile that I should bring.

In return you brought me kindness and care,
You held me tight and stroked my hair.
I held you like there was no tomorrow,
When I was with you I felt no sorrow.
That day I admitted how I felt,
I worried that I would go limp and melt.
Never before had I taken a step
That could bend and break what we have kept.
Then you took me into your arms,
You assured me that we are not harmed.
You told me that you knew we'd end
Up more than just the closest of friends.
Together we faced the toxic battle,
Of mocking, teasing and abusive prattle.
You wondered how I held my head so high,
I knew it was because you were by my side.
We were friends for fifteen short years,
Sharing our laughter and our tears.
Never did we think that life would be more cruel
Then even the bullies at our school.
I was not with you when you were told
About the cancer that would spread like mould.
Still, you remained incredibly brave,
Your courage did never waive.
For weeks and weeks you laid in bed
As into your veins you were fed
Chemo, drugs and 'shake and bake',
Still the cancer continued to take.
Until one day you pulled me aside,
And in my ear you did confide
No more strength in you did you hold,

It was your will to let fate unfold.
Together we met your parents and mine
And asked them to let the clock unwind.
They could see what I did not know,
I was not ready to let you go.
Forever fifteen is where you will stay,
While I grow old, tired and grey.
Forgive me for having trouble moving on,
My entire life has turned out wrong.
In my arms you took your final breath,
And from this world you passed into death.
I knew you were no longer in pain,
But also things would never be the same.
I think of you every single day,
And what our lives would be like if you did stay.
I wonder if we still would be
The closest that the world would see.
Now, the past grows very dark,
And pain and hurt has left its mark
But know that together we grew
And I owe my strength and courage to you.

NATURE'S PROMISE

Leslie Fern

A tiny seed laying on the earth, dormant but still
alive,
Waiting for the chance for its roots to grow and
thrive.
Reaching and stretching, pushing soil, making its
own way,
Carving its path to the air, to the light of day.

New life striving, building strength and sprouting
forth new limbs.
Trunks thicken and leaves form, reaching into the
wind.
Building up energy then letting it go as spring turns
away
As the heat builds up, the days grow long and the sun
spreads its rays.

Then autumn comes and weather grows cold as the
rains visit us all.
To hydrate and soften, wet the ground, to spread the
nutrients that fall.
Creating the vast branches of fruit, where hope is
stored
In seeds that drop to the ground, ready to grow life
once more.

STOP PLAYING WITH MY LIFE

Leslie Fern

You ask me questions, then ignore what I say,
You treat me like I'm weak, but I get stronger every day!
You claim it's for the best but how would you know
When it's my life you're playing with like it is fallen snow.
I am alone, more than most can even guess
Yet you pull on the strings and cut me from the rest!
You take all my hopes and put them in the bin,
You act with complete disgrace, anything to let you win.
I am struggling to survive while you work behind the stage
Increasing the pressure until I erupt into a desperate rage.
I am not your bloody plaything, a doll that you can pose
There is strength within this soul but you will not have it exposed.
Instead you put in place restrictions and barriers galore,
You expect me to just shut up as you hurt me and ignore
This pain, hurt, loneliness, this everlasting despair.
The isolation and hatred that builds up inside, do you even care?
It's not just me that you affect, your actions hurt others too

But know that there is a choice I things that you can
do.
Work with me, let me grow, don't ignore what I say,
Listen properly, compromise, Then you'll find I may
Know my limits and my strength is stronger than you
think
And together we can turn this corner and reform
these broken links.

GRADUATING WITH GRATITUDE

Leslie Fern

Today we reach the end of our lessons,
The road forward begins.
The coursework is done, the race has been won,
Now it falls to choices within.
We have each been in need of ways to think,
And now we need to act
To prevent the rebirth of wilfulness and rage,
To this we cannot go back.
This journey is one we have gone on together,
Forward in step and stride
We journaled the changes and worked on the skills
Which can keep our futures alive.
Still, this is one journey which none travel alone,
This is for certain, true.
Which is why on this day in gratitude
We say farewell, and thank you.

THESE HELPING HANDS

Leslie Fern

Whenever I am in need,
When I think I can't succeed,
There are things that I must do
To reinforce and renew
The commitments I made to myself,
To return my struggles to the shelf.
I must seek out help from those that care,
From those I know shall always be there.
I know it is hard to ask,
For me it is a challenging task.
But when a problem is shared around,
Facing it together is much more sound.
Challenge me, do not accept 'fine'
Push me to talk, let me unwind.
I may not find it easy to say
What is difficult, but I'll find a way.
Try not to minimise the strain,
It is hard to comprehend the pain,
Loneliness and fear I feel,
But this does not make it less real.
Do not rush but take the time,
Let me cry and let me whine,
For by this release I can get out
What the troubles are all about.
I am not used to people that care,
I'm more used to nobody's there,
So when someone is really near

I start to feel a very real fear
That another motive they possess,
Reassurance is the best.
Feel free to challenge me, I will listen,
Ignore the tears that soon may glisten.
The tears themselves do release
The pressure, loneliness and the grief.
So if you think I need a hand,
To lift me up and help me stand,
These helping hands are what's best
To leave my past and get some rest.

PHOTOGRAPHS

Leslie Fern

The click of a shutter
The whirring of gears
A brief interlude through
Two polished circles of glass
Capturing time in a single frame
Stopping movement and laughter,
Joy and celebration
An instant captured for eternity
Before time moves on
The moment lost
For ever more

THE NARROW RUTS

Leslie Fern

What is this building inside?
What is making me want to run and hide?
What is making my hands tremble so?
What is making my head say 'no'?
Why do I quiver in fear
when there is no danger near?
How can I face it when there's nothing to face?
How can I change it when I cannot place,
The turmoil, the stress, the churning gut?
I try to ride the narrow ruts
That are leading me to who knows where
Who knows what I'll find when I get there.
It is time to get some help,
To talk to someone, to build myself,
To share this load, to explore the black,
To move forward and never look back.

SANDS OF TIME

Leslie Fern

The sands of time flow through the glass
For all who are in the land
Take the memories, hopes and dreams
Lay them on the sands
The cycles of life ebb and flow
Bringing forth death and birth,
Creating the connections that support us all and
Reinvigorate the earth.
We are connected through junctions we know
And those we cannot see,
But if one is lost and not replaced
The rest cannot be free.
For throughout all time, the connections broken
Have left some people alone,
Without other persons upon whom to call
Upon the telephone.
We all seek company out for fun,
For relationships and as friends
To spend our lives and futures with,
And upon whom we can depend.
When connections are not found,
Time's passage slows and stalls,
As isolation sets in and
Life begins to crawl.
It's a painful cycle when
Friends cannot be seen,
For the world seems cruel and harsh
And life feels cold and mean.

So gather together your friends
And family upon whom you can depend,
For together the sands of time flow free
Onwards towards the end.
And our twinned hearts
Shall never, ever fall

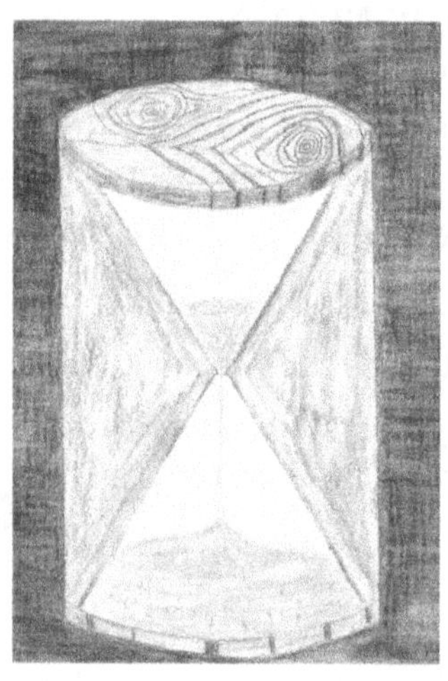

INTERTWINED

Leslie Fern

The touch of your hand
The beating of your heart
Two lives intertwined
Never far apart
My love for you grows
Expands outwards towards all

SELF

Leslie Fern

Gather
At the place where the mystery surrounds
The Ground
Upon which my body lays in state
Contemplate
The ways upon our life's work lays waste
In disgrace
Without the guidance and care of love and peace
At least
We can make our way to tomorrow where
The air
Can be as sweet as perfume and fresh as ice
Advice
Which I would give to my younger self:
To see
And be all I could be and never
Ever
Let those who mock you get you down.
Don't frown
But smile as hope can come from all.
Fall
And allow yourself to be helped to stand,
A man
Needs to learn that he cannot do it alone.
A home
Is not made for an audience of one.
The fun
Things in life are always shared.

Compared
To this we are lost in space.
With God's grace
We can do it all again
As Friends.

MY ANGEL

Leslie Fern

A heavenly blessing brought you to my side
My beautiful angel has come into my life
Filled my soul with beauty and grace
Taken my loneliness and put love in its place.
You walk beside me,
You let me stand tall
I love you, my angel,
And never shall it fall

FORTRESS

Leslie Fern

You build my heart into a fortress
You fill me full of strength
Your presence builds my soul
My love for you is boundless
Forever
Without end
You complete me

SOLITARY

Leslie Fern

Words cannot tell how I feel,
The pain is beyond what can be real.
When everyone I care for and love
Leaves me to rot in the fires above.
The remains of my heart, torn from my breast
And discarded with all the rest
Of my hopes, dreams, passions leaking away,
Leaving me feeling hopeless, alone and afraid.
Wishing for death's sweet kiss to silence my heart,
Separating the pain that has been from the start.
Knowing without doubt that I will be alone,
That there is no longer loved ones at home.
There is no other person on which I shall blame,
It is me who must feel the shame.
But I cannot handle all of this grief,
From this hurt I long for relief.
How long must I bear this weight?
How long until I settle this freight?
To drop this load I've borne since birth
Since I learnt how little I'm worth.
No one knows what lays deep inside me,
That I can never be all I wanted to be.
Dreams, hopes, passions now ignored,
Knowing my life is not worth fighting for.
Do I keep going even though I know the way,
Will lead to more pain and suffering each day?
Or do I seek the tender kiss farewell,

Knowing death will end this horrid spell?
I long for the time so long ago,
When there was one I gave my heart to so.
But those days are gone, so never look back
As my heart breaks with a final snap.

THE MIGRATION

Leslie Fern

Lightning flashes over the plains,
revealing the world far below,
Giving a sight
of zebra, elephant and hippo,
Dik dik, lion and giraffe
moving through the night.
For the message has been passed
from beak to snout, to mouth
spreading forth the word
of greener fields far away
beyond the mountain path,
just follow the morning bird.
So the great migration has started,
the animals have gathered around,
their journey has begun.
The swiftest birds lead the way
Giraffe follow and look around,
Waiting for the sun
To break through the dark night sky
And light the path for all below
To warn them of approach
Of the greatest predator of all,

The worst killer in history,
The slayer of most.
The poacher who kills without need,
The hunter without remorse,
Who kills because he can.
Who is this murderer,
The destroyer of all?
He calls himself man.
So be fleet of hoof,
Fly like the wind,
Spread word high and low
That the Great Migration has begun
The final race is underway,
Soon the elephant's call will blow.
The smallest and fastest quickly tire
Seek rest for a break
Upon a friendly back.
Here insects gather upon the skin
But the animals will clear them all
For a handy snack.
The animals spread far and wide
Each travelling with their kind
Across the dusty plain,
Always wary of the feline eyes
The padded foot and slashing claw
Of golden eyes and mane.
For man is not the only hunter
Out this day
Upon the beaten plains
As lions hunt for young and old
Taking those that fall behind

The sickly and the lame.
There are often ones who take
A life just begun
For a meal to feed their own
Foals and mothers both
To feed these golden ones.
But most animals will survive
To finish the great trek
Across the grassy land
To waters blue and trees of green
Beehives and termite mounds
Far from the burning sands.
But such paradise will not last
And time will quickly go
As days fade in the end
And nature's Great Migration,
This endless trek of animals
Will start once again.

WHEN I'M GONE

Leslie Fern

When I'm gone
Know I am always near
The chill in the air
The salt of the spray
The warmth of the flame
Know that I am forever watching
Observing, Knowing, Feeling
I forever shall be near

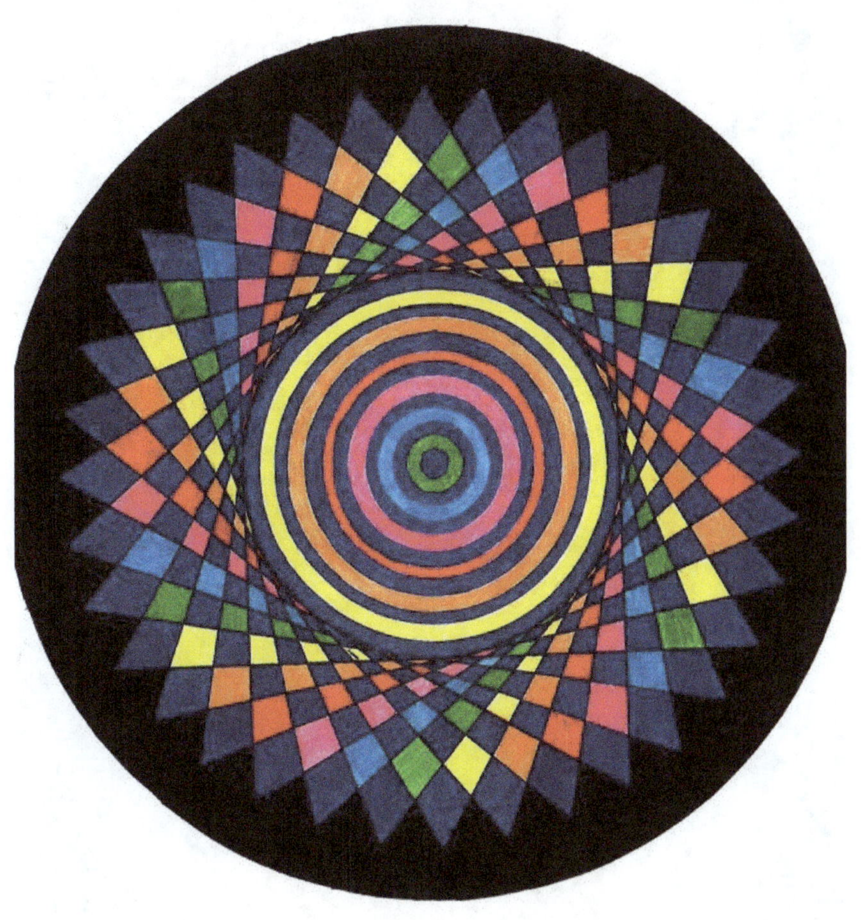

Rainbow Sunburst
Ink on Paper by Leslie Fern - 2025

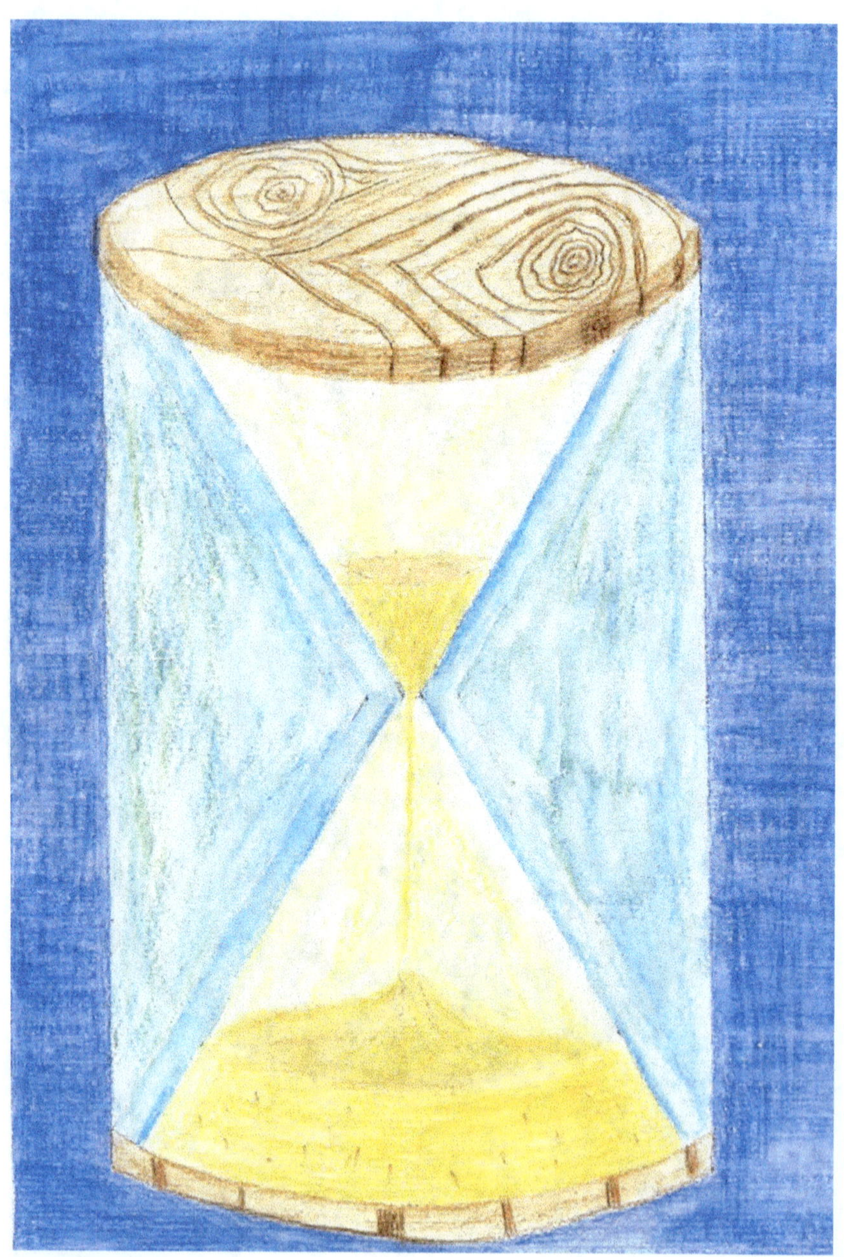

Sands of Time
Watercolour on Paper by Leslie Fern - 2025

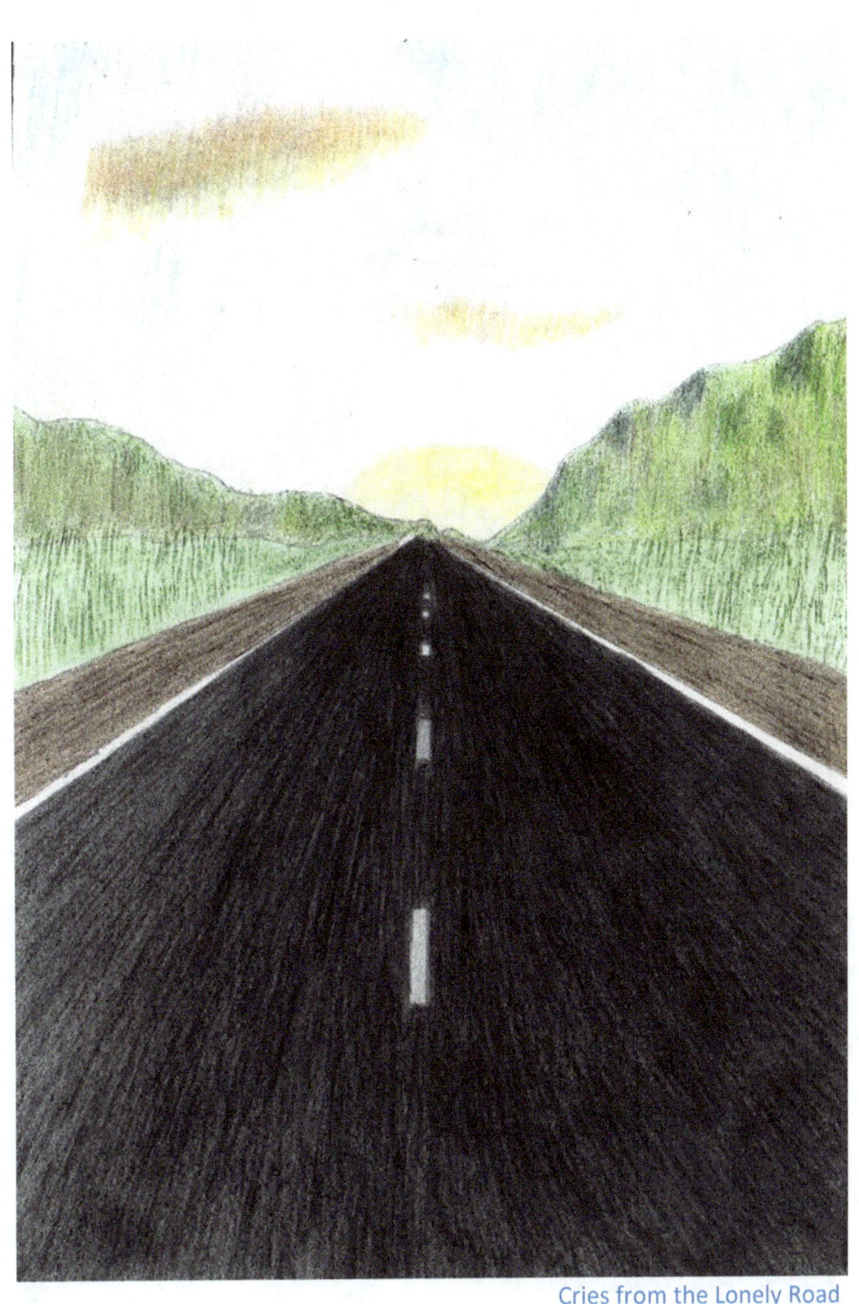

Cries from the Lonely Road
Pencil on Paper by Leslie Fern - 2025

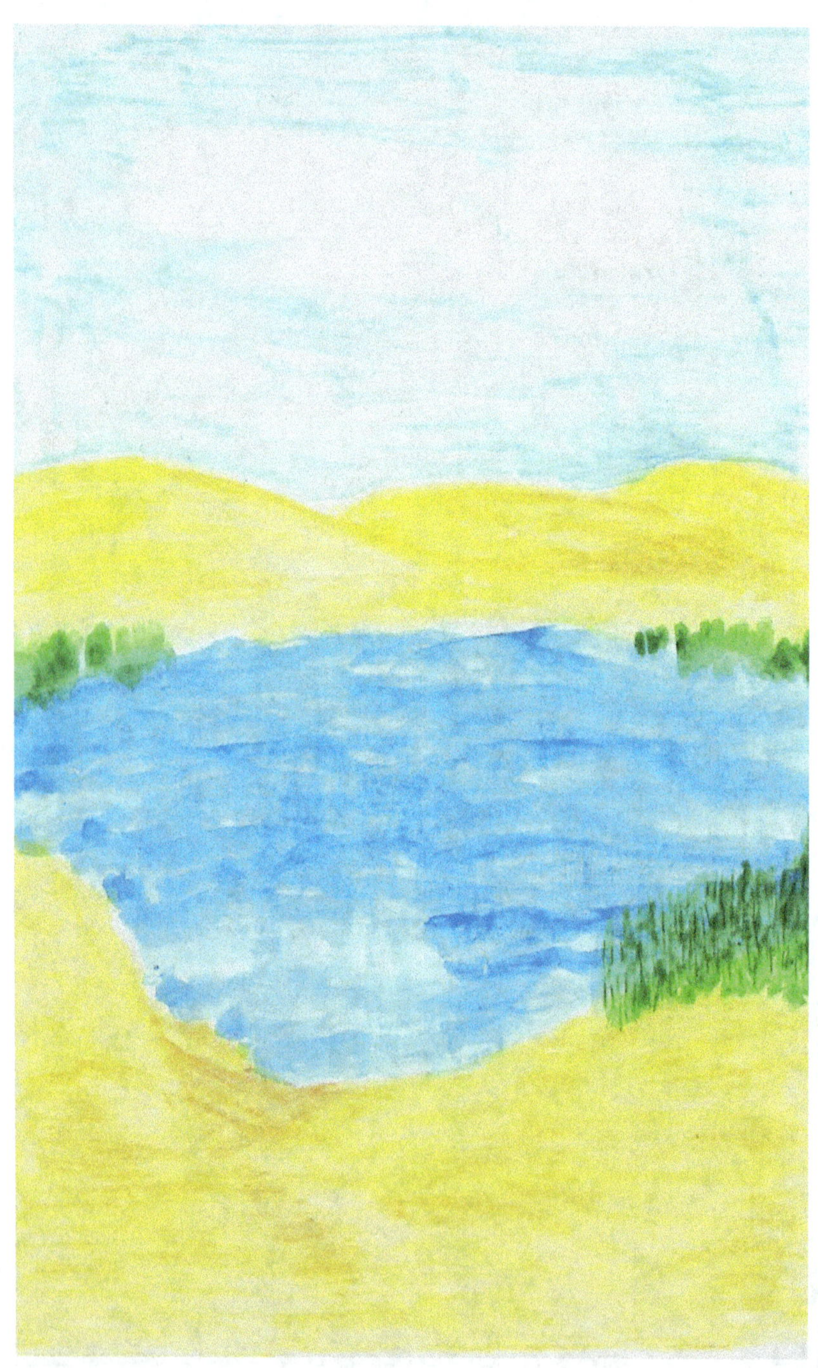

Oasis
Watercolour on Paper by Leslie Fern - 2025

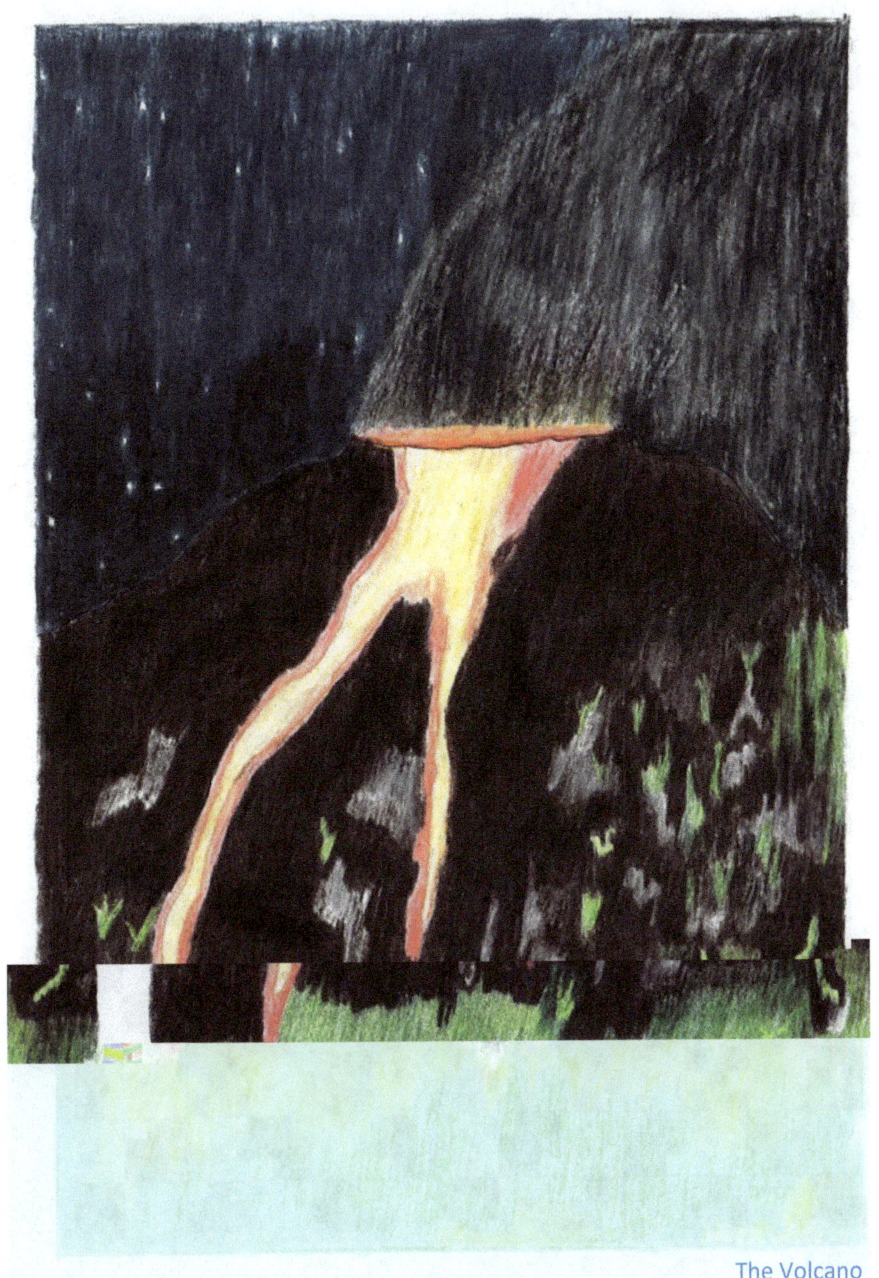

The Volcano
Pencil on Paper by Leslie Fern - 2025

This is Me
Ink and Pencil on Paper by Leslie Fern - 2025

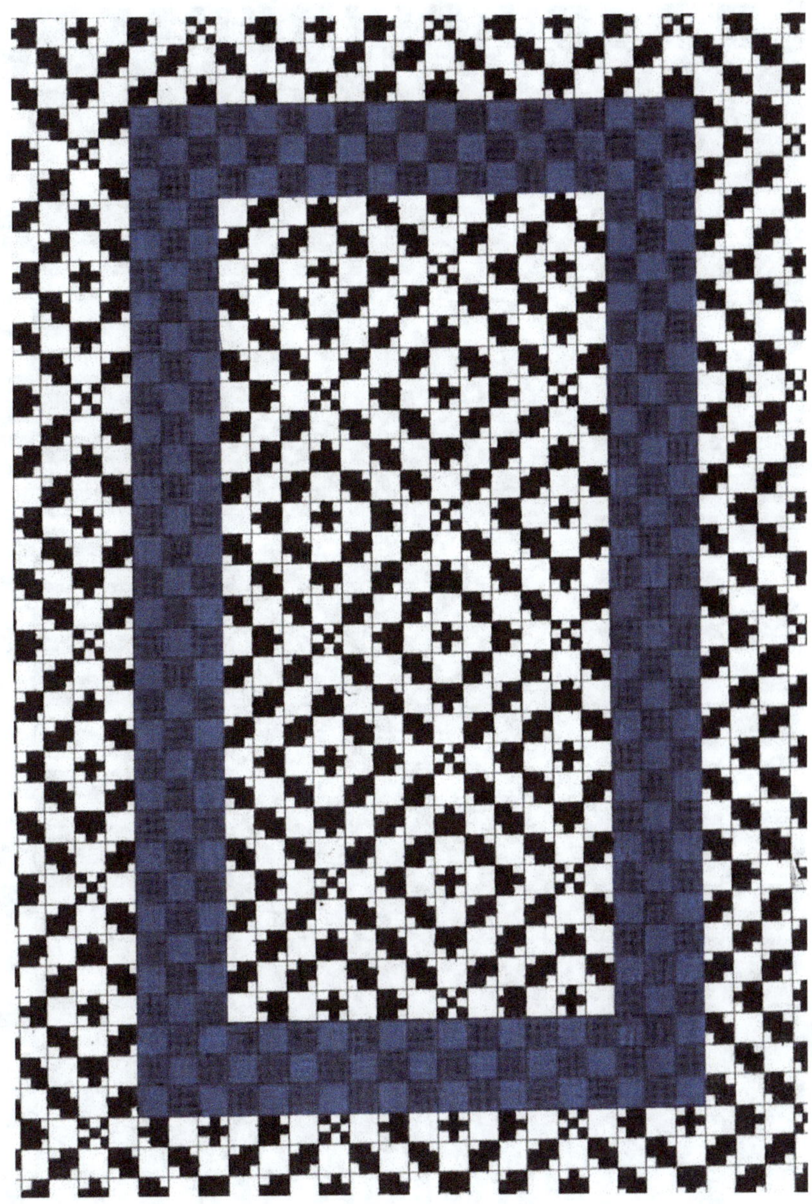

Straight from the Curves
Pen on Paper by Leslie Fern - 2025

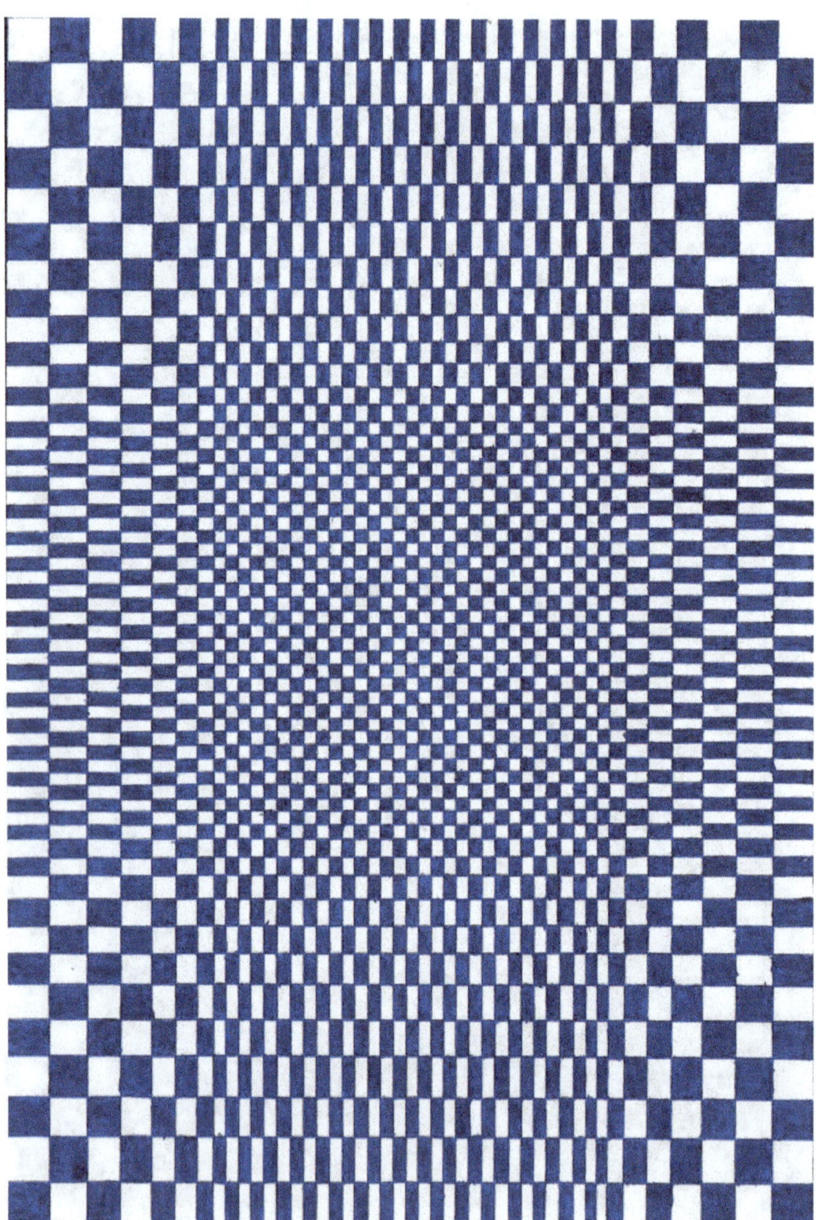

Sunken Oblong
Pen on Paper by Leslie Fern - 2025

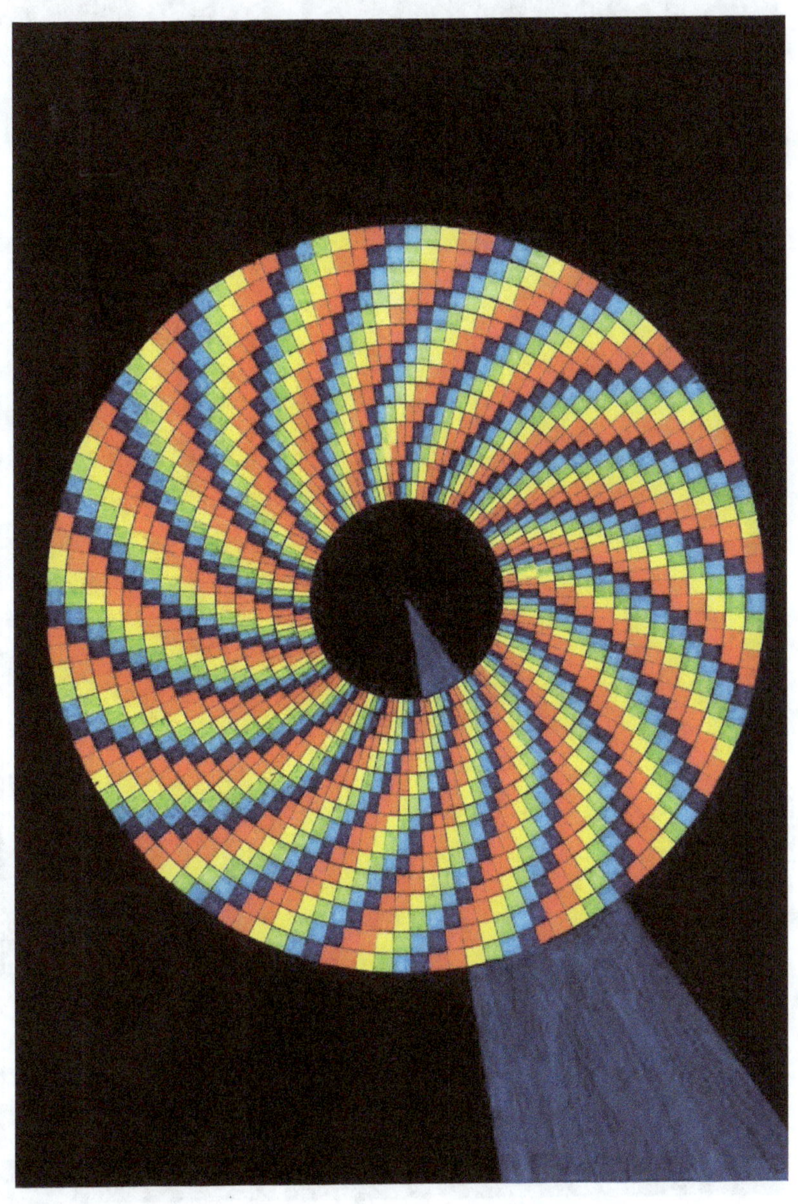

Rainbow Whirlpool
Ink on Paper by Leslie Fern - 2025

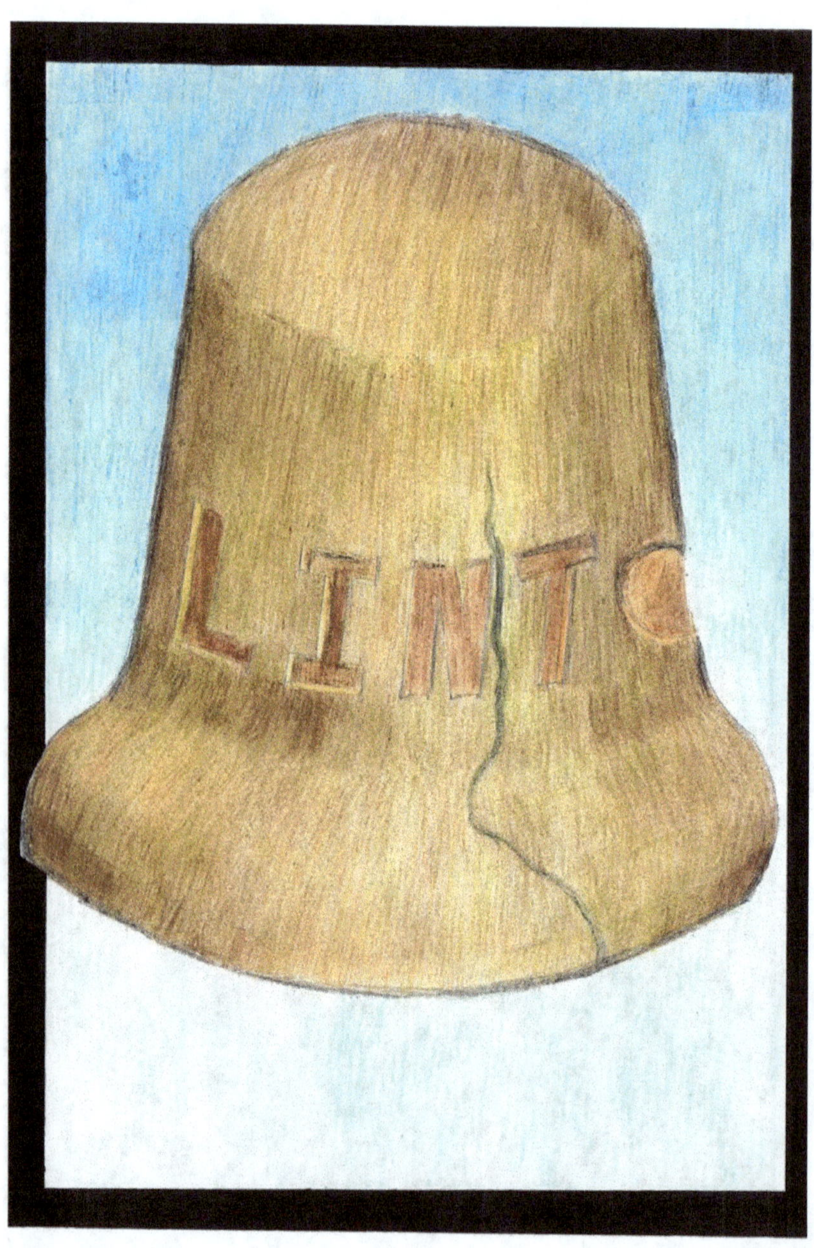

The Lonely Bell
Pencil on Paper by Leslie Fern - 2025

TAKE ME BACK

Leslie Fern

Take me back
To where the ocean floor
Shall be spread upon the shore,
And the secrets of happiness and truth
Were found within our youth.

Take me back
To when the worst fear
Was being kept down a year,
And the truths of fear and pain
Were hidden from me again.

Take me back
To when the mysteries of life
Are as fine as the edge of a knife,
And the hurt there is to bear
Can with loyal friends be shared.

Take me back

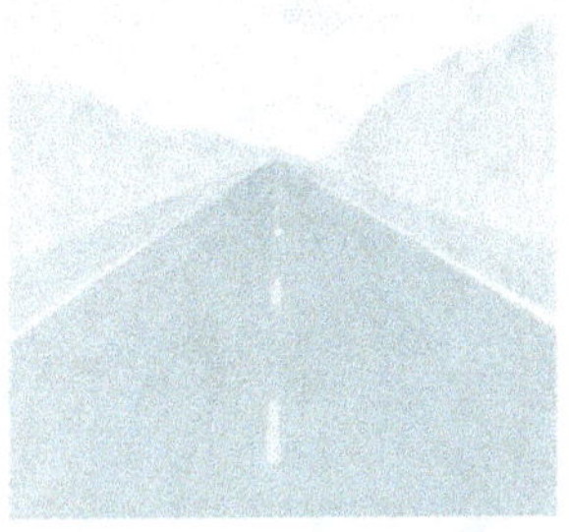

THE OASIS

Leslie Fern

An oasis hidden amongst the mounds,
Filled with the softest sounds,
Water and peace in ample abounds,
And happiness fills the air.

Not forever do these things stay,
Something sends into disarray,
The peace and happiness has gone away,
Shall it come again?

Is there one whose desire is true?
Whose heart is filled with love imbued?
Who accepts all others points of view,
And takes the common ground?

Let them bring back the life,
From the chaos and the strife,
Cut evil out with a knife,
And bring peace back once more.

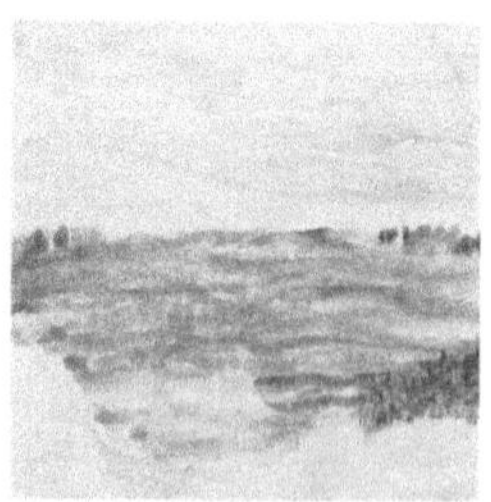

THIS IS ME

Leslie Fern

I cast my mind to where I can just be,
Where life could rise and thrive and play and sing,
Where I was told there was a place for me,
Where I can find I truly fit in.
But first I must choose where I do belong,
Which of the boxes I must choose to tick,
Although the answers both are simply wrong,
That neither of the choices want to stick.
So bravely I put down the poison pen,
And the board where on the form does stay,
I turn to those I can call my friends,
To them it is who I now do say:
Do not force me to bend, let me be free.
For people of this earth, this is me!

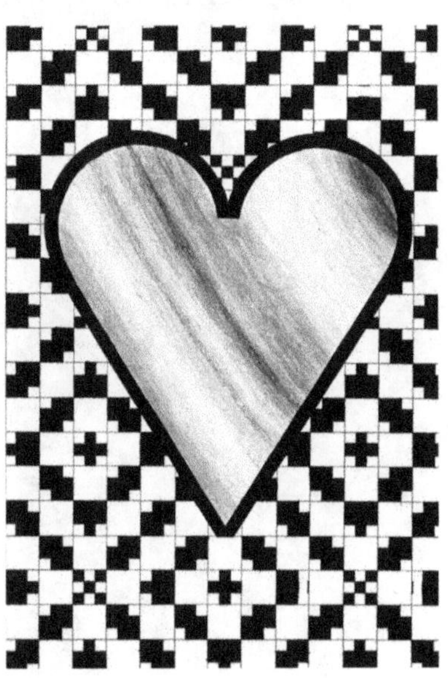

UNDERSTANDINGS

Leslie Fern

Understand that we love, we hope, we feel,
The chance to make the life we can begin,
The story where we toil without appeal,
For therein comes the secrets laying within.
Try make the story full of love at home,
Build all the tales of trust and prayers we plea
And help those who cannot help but feel alone.
Try to make them see that they are now free.
The hopeless youth that tear along and fight
Can now see that there is someone who is there,
Who loves and hopes that their future is bright,
For there is a chance for a gentle care,
So build your hopes and dreams on this delight,
For in life, you can find yourself tonight.

WHAT CAN BE DONE?

Leslie Fern

The same premise, whole countries at war,
Building up barriers and watching them fall
Thousands die at the turn of a hand
Murdered by their fellow man
Children run from the tracks of guns
Longing for the chance for fun
A chance to laugh and run and play
A chance to while away the day.
But where is fun when all you meet
Blood, buildings falling at your feet,
Whole families wiped out without a trace,
By proud members of the human race.
How can we sleep when terror abounds?
How can we eat when starvation mounds?
How can we succeed when we're surrounded by pain?
How can we trust leaders when they are to blame?
What can be done to protect our friends?
Try and make ourselves strong to the end.
Strong enough to face the tormentors from hell,
To strip the tyrants from the lies they tell.
Let's build it back and create an edge,
Let's make our lives an honest pledge.
Fight for those whose lives are torn apart,
And help them mend their broken hearts.

STAND UP AND STRIVE

Leslie Fern

What has happened to this world?
Has it gone insane?
Murder and mayhem have come to our shores,
Who is there to blame?
Youths run riot in the streets,
There are machetes and knives is hand,
This senseless violence has gone on too long
It's time to make a stand!
We are a brave and strong nation,
Being one and free our creed,
We welcome all with open arms
From those who face danger to those who have need
For refuge, safety, a stable home,
A place where their children can thrive,
A place where there is no corruption or fear,
A place to be alive.
But the safe place is no longer here,
For it, we all are worse.
A gathering to celebrate with the lighting of candles
Should never have need of a hearse!
Australia, we must stand up and strive
To take away this torment and fear.
We must never let this horror and murder
Take away all we hold dear.
Remember the 15 who have been killed,
Let their memories be our guide,
So light the light of hope and faith
and this terror will have nowhere to hide.

QUESTIONS

Leslie Fern

Who are the voices we cannot hear?
What would they say if they were near?
Would we stop to listen? Would they want to shout?
Would they think we heard all they talked about?
Where are they when the world has gone away?
Where do they go when the sky turns grey?
When can they speak? When will they be heard?
Why can we not learn what they in turn have
learned?
How can we ignore them? Let me ask you this,
How can we just turn away? Who knows what we'll
miss.
Who can you listen to and let them have their say?
Who knows what we can learn when we live this way.

LESSONS I'VE LEARNT (LETTER TO A BROTHER)

Leslie Fern

Hey there bro, yeah it's me
Who else you think it would be?
I have a lot that I want to say,
So, I'll tell you if I may.
You see, life has given me a second chance
To fight the fight, to dance the dance.
But I learned so much the first time round,
The lessons I learnt are now more sound.
I know I've hurt and been hurt as well,
Life often leads me to the gates of hell.
I am told I must persevere,
Easy to say when they are not here.
Hanging onto the bitter end
Is not easy without a friend.
I've lost most who I held dear
I've driven them far away from here.
I wish I could tell you that I was strong,
That I held true when all went wrong,
But that would be more than a lie,
It was my wish to lay down and die.
35 tabs went down with ease,
Swallowing them all was barely a squeeze.
But it seems that fate has other plans
As I woke up again in these bad lands.
I guess that I was lucky that in this hell
Was a man who could listen well.

He helped me reach out and talk to someone,
He did not judge me or make fun.
I never did get a chance to say
He saved my life when he acted that way.
I must admit that I still am broke,
For I do not heal like other folk.
But the thing I learned those fateful nights:
In order to win the battle I fight
I need to ask, beg and yell
Whenever I need somebody to help.
So, I finish this message to you,
With a whole new point of view.
Remember the lessons that I have learnt,
And know I'm here four you when you heart.
I may not be the greatest man
But I'll be here when you need a hand.
And know whatever happens in the end:
You are more than a brother, you're my best friend.

YOU COMPLETE ME

Leslie Fern

Hands holding
A lover's kiss
Nothing more in life do I miss
For you complete me
Like a budding rose
My love forever expands, it grows and grows.

PRIDE

Leslie Fern

The struggle is over, the battle begun,
The hardship stepped over, the race has been run.
You have crossed over the great divide,
When temptation appeared you did not run and
hide.
The battle you fought did not end in disgrace,
Yet you fought it with dignity and grace.
Still I know this much is true:
I am so very proud of you.
You are the reason I continue to try,
The reason our love will not die.
You are the reason I know and say
I am so blessed to be with you this day.

LIFE IS BEAUTIFUL

Leslie Fern

Building up hope in a world of rejection,
Making your mark with the sound of your name.
Gather the elements in the crucible of life and
Melt it all down with love's pure flame.

Shatter the past with the help of family,
Strengthen yourself from challenge of the day.
Polish your heart with companions and kindness
'Till it shines with blinding rays.

Don't fall to pieces when something fails,
It's bound to happen every now and then.
Pick yourself up and dust yourself off,
You can always count on the help of friends.

For when life gets rough, it always turns
Out for the best, it's how we learn.
When you build up strength and steady your pace
You can solve the problems that everyone's faced.

THE GREAT UNKNOWN

Leslie Fern

I lay in my bed, it's late at night.
Seems ages since I turned out the lights.
Sleep is such a fickle thing,
It flies from me as if on a wing.
I try to shut off my brain,
To ignore the fear and forget the pain.
My burden is mine alone to bare,
It cannot be easily shared.
It is not the dark I fear,
Although the dawn will soon be here.
Nor is it bullies I face,
I deal with them with patience and grace.
What I do fear is the great unknown.
When will I get to be at home?
Where will I soon lay down my head,
When these four walls no longer surround my bed.
Will I be able to finally be free?
Will I get the chance to be the real me?
So many questions with answers, none.
What should be exciting is no longer fun.
Thoughts and words swirl into the black,
The pace of them gets out of whack.
I make sure not to catastrophize
Or my fears will soon balloon in size.
Instead, I close my eyes and breathe.
See, I have another trick up my sleeve.
For in my head, I'm already free
And with everything else, what will be will be.

THE ENDLESS TRAIN

Leslie Fern

If I saw you today, would you recognise me?
Am I everything that you wanted me to be?
When you first saw me, could you tell
That keeping me would be a living hell?
When did you first decide
That you did not care if I lived or died?
When you decided to send me out
Did you not care to find out about
What has broken in the boy
Who once filled your life with joy?
Or, did you just pretend
And prayed and searched for an end?
Did you have a second thought?
Did your conscience leave you distraught?
Did you ever wish that you
Had a different point of view
Or are you happy that on that day
You made the choice to walk away?
I think of these things all the time.
When I realise you were the first in line
To walk away and not look back
A single carriage on the continuous track
From the endless train I look upon
Of people fleeing from this one.
Just another problem child
Who still has to live rand die
Knowing that everyone walks away
And do not care what they have to say.

THE VOLCANO

Leslie Fern

Sorrow is more than a toxic mess,
It is a volcano that forever vents.
Filling the land with poisoned gas
Into a world from which it cannot pass.
It occasionally goes to silent despair,
Soon, you forget that it's there.
But then it builds up, erupts
And the world becomes so rough.
Never does the sun's warm rays
Penetrate the cold, dark haze,
Instead all colour is drained away
And sorrow is here to stay.
One day something will plug the vent,
From where the gas once sent
Life far away from this poisoned land,
From where happiness is banned
To let joy return back in place,
And fill this soul with its grace.
It feels so long since I know
What it was that I could do,
To feel much more than this
Despair, sorrow, the thick dark mist
Of feeling so completely alone
And hundreds of miles from my home.
Where joy and laughter filled the days
And kept this sorrow far away.

FAMILY

Leslie Fern

It is more than bricks and mortar,
More than wood and stone.
It never has to give any quarter,
Nor seize a royal throne.
It covers more than grass or paper
Yet is as invisible as the cleanest glass.
It is as fine as the thinnest vapour,
Yet as strong as the thickest mast.
You find it where you least expect
And when it you do seek.
It is with those who demand respect,
And those who are quiet and meek.
What is this wondrous thing
that we cannot live without?
What goodness does it bring?
What is it all about?
Is it something we get for free
Or do we have to work?
Can it handle when we be
Nothing but a jerk?
It is something wonderful,
It is for you and me.
It is not ever 'uncool',
It is our family.

THE MOUSE TRAP

Leslie Fern

The bait is laid, the trap set.
No time for second thoughts or regrets.
Await the appearance of the mouse
Who thinks he can escape this house.
Await the snap, the broken back,
Throw it out and reset the trap.
My entire life feels like this,
Full of dead-end dreams and chances missed.
Built up hopes dashed into the ground,
Every right burned up without a sound
At the hands of power corrupt,
Those who've been given the public's trust
Followed on by 'for the public's safety'
My dreams destroyed by a Johnny-come lately
Who thinks they know what is best
By locking me away from the rest
Of humanity, alone, cold and afraid.
Unable to be myself and not somebody's slave.
A slave to 'treatments' that do more
Damage while real issues are ignored.
One day I will have too much
And things will then become too tough.
That is the day I give into truth,
The escape I longed for since my youth.
It is the only way I will be free,
When nobody can ever have control of me.
Until the ringing of that final bell
I shall suffer through this endless hell.

THOUGHTS

Leslie Fern

Every night as I lay in bed,
I hear the thoughts inside my head.
They multiply, go 'round and 'round,
They always appear without a sound.
At times when life is very rough,
When I feel I've had enough,
At these times my thoughts go dark
As despair hit's its mark.
I am told that things will change,
But like a dog infested with mange,
Every day I lose one more friend,
On whom I thought could not end
Or another bully gets to find
Another way to blow my mind.
'Sticks and Stones' is full of shit
Words do hurt and love to stick.
Soon others will pick up the call,
I struggle and try not to fall
As silent tears run down my face,
As I long to be far from this place.
Loneliness and fear are here to stay,
All my life it's been this way,
I guess that it is all I get,
A life of pain and deep regret.
I wish I could take back control
Of this lonely, tortured soul
But what can I do when the state itself

Leaves me to rot on this forlorn shelf.
I could have been more, much more so
But now we shall never know.
Forever, their claws in me will be
Until I can finally be free.

HOPES AND PLANS

Leslie Fern

I once believed there was some hope,
A plan that would help me to cope
With this life's ups and downs,
The cause of my pain and my frowns.
But as life has shown to me,
All my plans are not meant to be.
For as I learn each lonely day,
This pain and hurt is here to stay.
Destroyed by my own careless choice,
When I could not find my voice,
To ask for help can seem so wrong,
When my suspicions are too strong.
Too many times I Have been hurt,
Ignored, abandoned, even worse,
So trusting others is very tough,
And knowing this is very rough.
Others say for me to ask
For their help when I face a task
Or problem that is too tough to bare.
I try to get my mind back where
I challenge myself to push my walls,
To do what I feel is the hardest call

But when things are tough I find
Thoughts and doubts confuse my mind.
This is when I am too meek,
When my voice is far too weak
So I must do these things now
While my back is tough and I know how
To let you know that I need help,
And I cannot do this by myself.

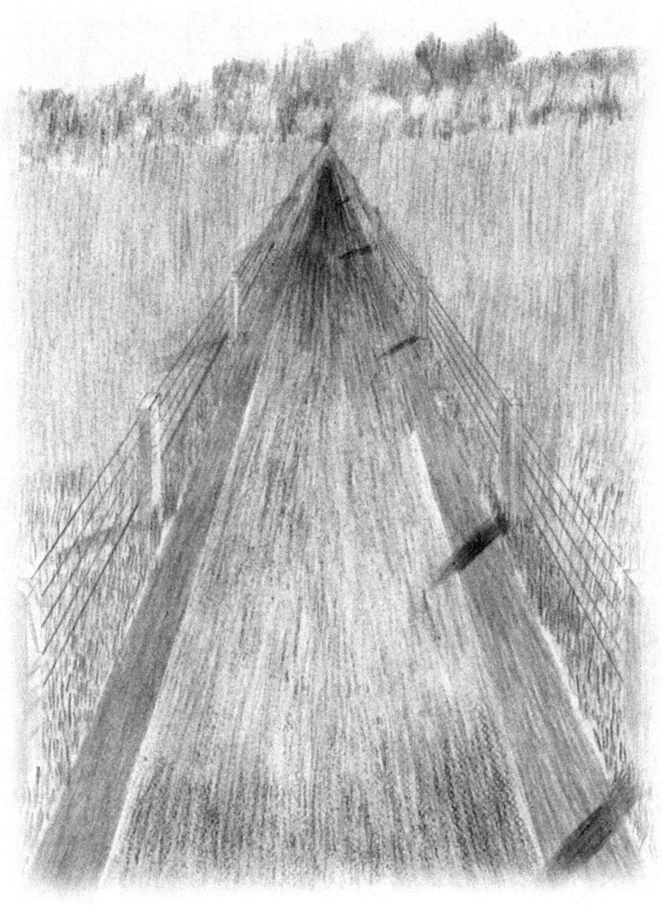

LONELINESS

Leslie Fern

What can I do when my dreams have died?
When the punishment becomes unjustified?
I'm not the type to yell and scream,
I cannot imagine being mean.
It's not a person that crushed my spirit,
There is not a person who would hear it.
Instead this country that I love
Has torn out what once laid above.
It crushed my soul when I was small,
It raised me up and let me fall.
But these days did never end,
Soon I found I had no friends.
I wish I could understand my brain,
Maybe then I could stop this pain,
But each time I take off the cover,
Each dark layer is followed by another.
So, I keep my head down and wear this mask
And pray this pain might soon will pass.

I AM ME BECAUSE OF YOU

Leslie Fern

When struggles drag me to the ground
When I feel no one is around
When pain tears me apart
You help me mend my broken heart
When fear leads me astray
When I don't know what to say
When hope is gone, when I'm alone
You welcome me into your home
When sorrow fills me to the bone
I know that I am not alone
You are there, with outstretched hand
To help me be a better man
You build me up when I am down
You turn my life upside down
I know this much is true
I am me because of you

LAUGHING AND CRYING

Leslie Fern

No one cared yet all could see
Troubles build inside of me
No one helped this little child
Made me laugh or made me smile
I was left on my own
To face the monsters at my home
Nightmares lurked in from the dark
Happy and ready to leave their mark
I put on a mask so nobody can know
The pain that lives deep inside me so
Aching fills me to the bone
As I'm torn away alone
I try to do my very best
To hide the pain from the rest
I can only wonder why
I do not go and run and hide
When there's pain it always builds
Deep inside the heart it fills
It tears the soul from its shell
Condemning me to a world of hell
Looking to where I can turn
For the home and love I yearn
But there is no one to call
So from my eyes the tears still fall

LONGING FOR HAPPY DAYS

Leslie Fern

We were young and we were free
There was nothing we could not be
Many thought that we were blessed
Living our lives to the best
When you were here we had it all
A love so strong it could never fall
But life is cruel in many ways
I long for those happy days
Struggling through these lonely days
Struggling through this awful pain
I remember your face, I remember your name
If you were here would you do the same
Then death tore us apart
Split us up and broke our hearts
Memories fade as time goes on
The love you have will one day be gone
If you have that special one
One that makes your love so strong
Enjoy each moment you spend with them
Because you don't know when it will end

A HOLLOW HEART

Leslie Fern

I sit here with a hollow heart,
Waiting for my life to start.
Wishing for a solid core,
Leaving me wanting more.
I wish that others would reach out
But, like an angry wasted shout,
I am feeling all alone
With no place to call my home.
So many times I try to call,
With no ears upon which to fall.
Instead U an pushed to the side,
As others simply try and hide.
Whatever happened to families are forever,
And siblings being there together?
This black sheep has long been shorn,
All connections have been torn.
How am I meant to make some friends
When every friendship is forced to end?
So many simply have pulled the plug,
Leaving with feelings smug
As they move onto calmer seas,
Not caring at all what happened to me.
I must now face the facts:
There is no turning back.
Loneliness is now a friend,
At least this friendship will never end.
It is time to accept the past,
Relationships simply do not last.

I'm condemned to be alone,
With only loneliness to fill my home.
Perhaps one day this will change,
And my heart will be in range
Of those who accept me for me.
This is the day I shall be free.

ANGER

Leslie Fern

Continual anger takes a toll,
On the body, the mind, the soul.
It wears you down to the core,
It leaves you wanting something more.
It makes you weary from its drive,
Leaves you being forced to strive
For a break from the strain
As it digs its claws into your brain.
This soul of mine needs to rest
If I am to give my best,
But where do I lay this blame,
Betrayal, hurt and the shame.
If I leave it deep, it will grow,
Spread and corrode me, so
I must release this dark black mist.
I'll leave it where it won't be missed,
For then I can start anew
With a much brighter point of view

IMAGINATION

Leslie Fern

There is a seed deep inside my soul,
A tiny speck within the whole.
It germinated when I was small,
When I was barely a half metre tall.
It grew from tales of dragons and knights,
It was moulded by sounds and sights.
It was always hidden, never seen
'less it was thought to be obscene.
It shaped my world by night and day,
It keeps the loneliness far away.
It took on a life of its own,
It made itself at home.
For so long it sought release,
To expand, grow, to give me peace.
For so long I locked it tight
As I hid away in fright.
But now it can emerge and shine
As I find a place and time
Where I now can be seen and heard,
To help me soar, fly like a bird
To share its presence, so all can see
The beauty that lives deep within me.
It now gives me strength and relief
From my pain and my grief
It creates stories and paintings, made
With colour and hope from courage paid
It is now that I can finally see
How incredible my imagination can be.

LESSONS

Leslie Fern

I wake each day
The exact same way
Forever ignoring the pain that stays
I bide my time
And continue the climb
While my emotions are in decline
I wonder if each
Time that I reach,
I can take in these lessons they teach
Or will it instead
Go over my head
And stew my mind when I go to bed
I ask for a hand
To help me to stand
And let me be with my fellow man
But whenever I do
It feels so new
Like a seed before it grew.
But, now I know
This seed has grown
And my strength is building, and so
I will keep on moving
For life is grooving,
All my fears and sorrow it's soothing
And tomorrow I shall
Be able to tell
Of these lessons that I now know well.

MY WRITINGS

Leslie Fern

Words swirl inside my mind,
Letters jumbled then fall in line.
Seeking others to join their form,
Building like a gathering storm.
One after another, the lines emerge,
At times in a trickle, at times with a surge.
Building each upon the last,
Telling stories of a tougher past.
Each time, I write without a plan,
These poems emerge any way they can.
At times they express an unspoken angst,
Or a challenge I'm up against.
I let my mind go where it may,
And let my feelings have their say.
I do not filter through these thoughts,
Instead I find lessons to be taught.
Each poem I finish, I share it around
For others to read, their opinions to sound.
This way I can hone my art
And build up strength within my heart.
Many I turn to for advice,
Knowing at times the truth is not nice
Some lessons are hard to learn,
Some embers can still burn.
But I know that they mean well,
And it is with honesty that they tell,
So I write and share and send
And hope it help us in the end.

NIGHTMARES

Leslie Fern

Dark dreams swim through my mind,
Sending my thoughts back in time
To places I wish I did not know,
To times where I don't want to go.
My heart races and my pulse quickens,
The dark mists start to thicken
Torment racks through my brain,
Threatening to send me insane.
What nightmares disturb my sleep?
The old stories that still make me weep.
So much pain and so much hate
Leave me unable to concentrate.
I wish these dark dreams would stop
Turning my brain into knots,
Disrupting my sleep and leaving me drained,
As I remember the anguish and pain.
There was so little I could do back then,
As the cycle repeated again and again.
One by one the dominos fall,
'till none are left standing tall.
I know now I must take the chance,
To reach out my hand and dance this dance.
To turn these nightmares 'round again
And fill my future with family and friends.

PRECIOUS ONE

Leslie Fern

Precious one, still yet to bloom,
Why do you drown in gloom?
So much beauty in you that you hide,
When others would falter, you continue with pride.
Your strength grows and builds within,
Still your journey is yet to begin.
Who can foresee the battles you'll face,
Except that you'll face them with dignity and grace.
You'll never face an impossible quest.
You'll fight a great fight and give all your best.
Precious one, times will get tough.
Life will be cruel and it will be rough.
You will lose loved ones along the way,
So many close friends you will wish would stay.
There shall be times you'll feel all alone
When there's no answer on the telephone.
You'll feel as if you have no friends.
You'll cry and beg for the pain to end.
At these times you must be strong,
You'll persevere and carry on.
Precious one, I close with this,
An important lesson that must not be missed.
Although your journey may feel so hard,
There will be help to fill in your card.
Even with the hardest task,
You'll receive assistance when you ask.
Together you shall achieve the goal,
The amazing beauty within your soul.

That is where your true strength lies,
Within your heart that never dies.

THE SHARPEST EDGE

Leslie Fern

Why when I am getting strong, do I still seek out
pain?
Is there something wrong with me? Is my past to
blame?
There are so many things that are beyond my control,
Yet so much turmoil lies deep within my soul.
There are parts of me that yearn for a blade,
The sharpest edge, the running blood where the scars
are made.
I know these cuts run deep, they carve me to the
core,
But something down deep inside leaves me wanting
more.
It is hard to fight this temptation, but still I know I
must
Work up my courage and let someone know, I must
learn to trust.
The marks I wear are not easily seen, I make sure of
that
But if I continue upon this path, there'll be no turn-
ing back.
So, this is how I'm asking for help to solve this prob-
lem that I face,
And together we can solve this riddle and return san-
ity in its place.